1973

79 828

INHERIT
YOUR OWN
MONEY

Other books by Elmer Otte

REHEARSE BEFORE YOU RETIRE

RETIREMENT REHEARSAL GUIDEBOOK

WELCOME RETIREMENT

INHERIT YOUR OWN MONEY

An Exciting New Concept in Retirement Planning

Elmer Otte

DAVID McKAY COMPANY, INC.
New York

Library of Congress Cataloging in Publication Data

Otte, Elmer.
  Inherit your own money.
  Bibliography: p.
  Includes index.
  1. Retirement. 2. Retirement income. I. Title.
HQ1062.082   301.43′5   78-13201
ISBN 0-679-51100-8
ISBN 0-679-51101-6 pbk.

1 2 3 4 5 6 7 8 9 10
Manufactured in the United States of America

To Margaret and our children,
as much for their challenges
as for their encouragement.

Contents

Preface

The premise for *Inherit Your Own Money* comes from the people: from the people in modest apartments and grand condominiums; from those who stayed in back-home communities, and others who moved to palm-shaded retirement communities. It comes from hundreds of challenging research visits I have had with retired and elderly persons around the country, and beyond.

These seasoned citizens keep insisting that money is not quite the retirement bugaboo they had worried about, in spite of rising costs and inflation, and our uncertain economy. They find the money they actually have to live on and the income they *really need* for retirement living are both a different, and more favorable, reality than most had imagined.

Their biggest *fear* before retirement was always whether they would have enough money to live on. Would it last for the rest of their lives, and would it be enough to take care of them during illnesses and in old age? The *realities* with which they live out their lives are quite different from all these concerns.

They are surprised to find that they still accumulate new money: they keep saving more money, even after job and career incomes have stopped. Surprising numbers confide that they are actually enjoying more take-home and keep-home income than had been the case while they were still employed.

Sure, things cost more and prices keep skyrocketing, and inflation waters down our bundle. But we can expect retirement income amounts to keep growing, too, since some of that income is indexed to the cost-of-living increases we live with. Also, many assets keep appreciating, and most of us continue to generate more new income.

As an author of preretirement planning books and study materials, and as a lecturer on aging and retirement living, I receive supportive advice and also common sense from these people. They suggest that I warn those others who are approaching their later years to be wary of "living poor and then dying rich." They report having been so filled with money fears themselves and living so poor in spirit, that they seldom noticed all of the wonderful choices they still had open to them. Choices like being willing to invade "rainy day money" at times when things really "begin to pour."

You can decide to keep on enjoying and appreciating what can be life's happiest times. And it is not necessary that you start spending all of your money. You should not spend too much too fast, either. What I do recommend is a sensible factoring of income expectations and some assets to cover the costs of living, for a higher enjoyment of the rest of your lifetime.

We do indeed have choices, but choices like these require conscious decision-making.

Inherit Your Own Money echoes the wise voices of people from a wide spectrum of fiscal and family circumstances. This is a report of their experiences. It is also a philosophy to guide the job of coping with the cost of growing older.

Like the toast says: "May you live as long as you want, and never want for as long as you live."

Introduction

This book is about hope—hope for mid-career people still approaching retirement, and for older, already retired people. It is true that inflation is eating us alive, with taxes and high prices licking up much of what is left. If you are mid-career, you are probably beginning to have nightmares. For those who are retired, these nightmares are in full color and illustrate their health concerns, financial worries, and job and career fears. Yet, there is hope; we have choices we seldom acknowledge. Look at all those middle- and upper-income individuals and couples, and look, as well, at the widowed and the divorced. Many of these people live careful lives, and end up leaving estate residues of surprising amounts.

Facing the New Realities

We live in a fluid time—a time of fast changing social circumstance. Much that was sacred yesterday is today being questioned, or ignored. Increasingly, we face the hard fact that concern about the future is no longer about "leaving something for them." It is now, increasingly and irrevocably, about "keeping something for us." We are going to continue to come up against an expanding number of surprising new realities, such as:

(1) Most of us can expect to retire earlier and live longer. We will, therefore, need to use up more of our assets for our own comfort and security during our longer lifetime.

(2) Taxes have become the relentless leveler of society. In our country and around the world taxes are the sure-fire vehicle for redistributing both our assets and our income.

(3) Psychiatrists like my friend, Dr. Keith Keane, (of Wisconsin and Arizona) insist that parents should not leave too much of their net worth to their children—neither too much, nor too soon. Inherited wealth dulls their sense of struggle, weakens survival instincts, and lays the foundation for much future guilt and depression.

(4) Life expectancy is approaching eighty and beyond for those not yet 60. With a life expectancy of more than 15 years for anyone at age 65, we should reach and pass 80 years of age—and by that time our children should be from 50 to 60 years of age themselves. If they haven't made it by then, heaven help them, and us.

(5) As science continues stretching out the average life expectancy, the customs and economics of employment (regardless of official retirement ages) keep shrinking the years we are expected, or permitted, to work at our careers. This generation of leisure necessitates, to a certain extent, that part of our inheritance be used to finance our extra years.

(6) The acquisition of new income does not cease with retirement, and, naturally, the accumulation of new assets during our post-employment years startles many older persons. We are living in an age of mounting social security and pension payments for everyone. Very often these new sources of guaranteed income have cost-of-living increases built in, enabling us to keep in step with most of inflation's bite.

(7) Society may protest against mandatory retirement, and Congress may keep stirring that brew, but Social Security administrators tell me that more than half the working force takes their social security at age 62, and 60 percent are already taking it before they reach age 65. The fact that more are retiring earlier says a great deal about our real attitudes about hanging-on, or hanging-it-up. (Also, having more than one career is the new wave.)

(8) Children are no longer expected or required to provide for parents who become dependent; society, through its welfare system, now carries that burden. Church tithing (in most faiths) is

all but dead, with the traditional 10 percent having been cut to half or less, possibly because society (utilizing our taxes) shoulders a bigger share of citizen needs. What this means is that social welfare is just one more cushion against our fear of disaster.

(9) Contemporary Western society has for generations, and even for centuries, not been permitting its members to perish from starvation. Whenever real hunger is acknowledged, society rallies 'round with relief. We need not fear going hungry.

(10) Most of us, even the modest accumulator, will be worth much more at death than we ever realized or acknowledged during our lives. Our appreciated property and assets immediately become accountable—and taxable. Our leftovers are redistributed, and are probably taxed again. *And then they are spent—by others.*

(11) For the first time in our history, an increasing number of middle and upper income people are able to project ahead and program their income expectations to pay for their later years. They can depend on financing those later years from guaranteed income from optional sources of new money and from the asset income earned on their savings. It is possible, today, to match your life expectancy with your income, and to judiciously invade your principal, without ever depleting all assets or income for living.

Inherit Your Own Money is neither a solution to the problems of the elderly poor, nor a message about their condition. This book is, instead, a promise and an upbeat program of hope for those who have always tried to manage, look after, and cope with, their own problems—and their own opportunities.

Acknowledgments

Many people encouraged the idea of this book, and many others provided insights and data, for which I am most grateful. I will not be able to mention or even, perhaps, remember them all, but I do especially wish to acknowledge these several: Charles Lingelbach, Dr. Keith Keane, John Zimmerman and Harold Adams of Appleton, Wisconsin, who helped spark much of this concept; Donald Cutler and my agent, Dominick Abel, of New York, and my son, David Otte of Boston, who nurtured and encouraged my pursuit and progress; Skip Lange of Indianapolis, Joe Sperstad of Milwaukee, Marion Cranston of Minneapolis, Mary Agnes Truttschel of Hixson, Tennessee, and Jerry Jolin of Galveston, Texas, all of whom pushed me forward or provided anecdotal content. Then there are Dr. Norman Vincent Peale and, of course, my own pastor and writing friend, Father Jim Putman; and Saul Gruner, New York, Joe McCarthy of the Life Insurance Institute in Washington; and John Rosebush, Owen Lyons, Neil McCarty, Vince Derscheid, Bud Schuetter, Cam Woyak, June Zwickey, Gloria and Lyle Hoeft, Judy Boncher, Phyllis Gauger, Vic Zaremba, Ed Arthur, Milt Ness, Jackie Nytes, Hal Phillips, Ray Sauvey, Will Allmandinger, Carlos Seville, Phil Keller, Charles Lageman, Bill Desing, Phil Schlichting, and Ken Houts, Louis DeGrace, Cy Puetz, Peter Fritzell, the Hoopers, Dr. Kurt Dietzler of Marburg, Germany, and so many others both near and far.

I am also grateful for permissions granted, for the use of data and materials created by others which has appeared in media including newspapers serviced by the Field Newspaper Syndicate, the *Retirement Rehearsal Guidebook,* published by Pictorial Publishers;

Rehearse Before You Retire, by Retirement Research; the *Milwaukee Journal;* the *Minneapolis Tribune, Christian Science Monitor; Better Homes and Gardens; Family Health* and *Reader's Digest* magazines; and the *New York Times.* I am especially grateful for the many wonderful, inspiring articles which have appeared in *Dynamic Years, Retirement Living,* and *Modern Maturity,* and to the creative writers who wrote these stories. Drs. Bernice L. Neugarten and Karol K. Weinstein, and their research data which was compiled by Robert C. Atchley in his second edition of *The Social Forces In Later Life,* has been most helpful; as has so much which the late Gerald Loeb wrote and espoused about judicious consumption of principal. I also acknowledge writers I have read and quoted, professionals like Tom Collins and Sylvia Porter.

I would be remiss if I were to overlook the guiding hands of Rainelle Peters, my editor, and Alan Tucker, the executive vice president of David McKay Publishing Company.

INHERIT
YOUR OWN
MONEY

1

How to Live It Up —Down to Zero Estate

If your riches are yours why don't you take them with you to the other world
BENJAMIN FRANKLIN
Poor Richard's Almanac

Inherit Your Own Money is about de-cumulation. It is about using your net worth assets to help finance the rest of your increasingly longer lifetime. The key to this premise is your life expectancy.

Both the messages and the methods examined here come from real-life people, couples and individuals who have been managing their "rewarding years" reasonably well. This book will show how you can manage your life, and how to program the use of your assets so that *you* will get to enjoy the fruits of your labors, without getting into a cold sweat about whether your money will last as long as you do.

Most of us have a difficult time acknowledging the comforting presence of our own prosperity. We are apologetic about being nice to ourselves. We grow so skilled at living poor, especially in spirit, that we end up dying rich. And we never notice until it is too late that we have always had so many happy choices.

We often dedicate our hardworking lives to the careful, and endless, accumulation of assets. We become so accomplished and proud

1

of our thriftiness that it never occurs to us how or when to begin reversing the process. No wonder it has often been said that long life, success, and the so-called golden years of retirement are wasted on old people.

Gerald Loeb, the late, leading Wall Street investment analyst and writer, advised older people to forget about leaving a lot of money to heirs, and to live it up a little in these high-cost days by invading capital judiciously. He favored digging into capital in some cases to give the elderly added pleasures—eating out more often, joining clubs for social involvement, taking trips during dreary winter months, going out for entertainment, making visits to children—activities which might otherwise strain regular monthly budgets.

Loeb's method urged the elderly to consult insurance acturial tables and figure their life expectancies. Then, he said, they should double their expected remaining number of years to obtain the fraction by which they could prudently use up capital—safely.

Table 1 is the life expectancy table used by the Equitable Life Assurance Society, which covers the years from age sixty-five to eighty-five.

Checking with this life expectancy chart, and following the Loeb premise, you will find, at age sixty-five, that you can expect to have fifteen-plus years left to live and enjoy. Loeb suggests we double this number and invert it,

$$\frac{1}{15 \times 2} = \frac{1}{30}$$

and that *we can then safely use up capital* at the rate of one-thirtieth each year without ever running out of money. If your total capital balance were $100,000, for example, you could safely draw down $3,333.33 *of principal* per year for the rest of your life without ever running out of capital. This may not quite get you down to zero estate, but it should be a lot more acceptable to those of us who fear running out of money. (In addition to the principal, you may also use *the earnings*.)

It is also now a fact that many of our continuing and future needs for income are cushioned by a variety of guaranteed and otherwise assured income sources and systems. One of the most widely accepted

Table 1

Age	Expected remaining years	
	Male	*Female*
65	15.92	19.11
66	15.24	18.30
67	14.53	17.50
68	13.93	16.71
69	13.29	15.94
70	12.67	15.18
71	12.07	14.44
72	11.47	13.72
73	10.90	13.01
74	10.34	12.33
75	9.80	11.66
76	9.27	11.02
77	8.76	10.39
78	8.27	9.78
79	7.80	9.19
80	7.35	8.63
81	6.91	8.08
82	6.49	7.56
83	6.10	7.05
84	5.72	6.56
85	5.36	6.10

methods of "eating your own seed corn" without ever running out is actually a very conservative and risk-free process.

This method is called the joint-and-survivor annuity, which pays you a set monthly income for life, with the surviving spouse continuing to get a percentage (usually two-thirds of the guaranteed amount). The case illustrated here is from the experience of a very real and not too unusual family situation. It is the Peterson experience.

Chet Peterson's parents were reaching the ages of sixty-nine and seventy at the time that they became acutely aware that they weren't getting around or managing very well anymore. (The

*children had noticed it too.) There were anxious family confer-
ences about whether the senior Petersons could or should remain
in their own home and how, in the face of their new circumstances, their property and money should now be managed. Two
daughters and a son, all married and involved in careers of their
own, worked it out and agreed together about what their parents
should do.*

*The old folks were understandably apprehensive about having
sufficient income coming in, and were upset about health and
housing concerns. So it was decided to help them sell off everything to cash in all of their assets, and then to invest all the cash
remainders–including the conversion of cash values of their considerable life insurance–into one large single premium, joint-and-
survivor annuity.*

*Their fine old family home was sold at an appreciated profit
and they also disposed of most of the fine old family things it had
been filled with. They cashed in invested assets, some at attractive
capital gains. Their life insurance policies were simply converted
into one big new annuity. Everything was liquidated and consoli-
dated according to the sound plan and cautious advice of Chet
Peterson, their only son, who was a life insurance actuarial professional.*

*The Petersons moved into comfortable apartment housing,
secure in the knowledge that their estate had added up to a very
surprising $200,000. This amount was now safely invested in a
lifetime annuity for both of them, providing an income they could
not outlive.*

We may gasp a bit about the size of the Peterson pile, but you will
soon learn that amounts like these are not all that uncommon today.
You may also be upset about the idea of putting that much money,
practically their entire estate's net worth, into just one investment,
even if that one source is providing a lifetime annuity. Naturally, this
will not be the happiest, not even the best solution for everyone. It is a
sound answer for the Petersons, because it removed their anxieties
about whether their money would last.

It gave them enough income to cover practically any life style
they chose, with enough left over to cover uncertainties and even to
insure against health catastrophe.

How much monthly income is guaranteed in such a lifetime annuity?

The Peterson annuity began immediately to pay them an income of $1,450 per month which totaled $17,400 in annual income. Their specific annuity is payable until both are deceased, with the survivor getting two-thirds for life, and with ten years of certain income arriving in any case.

That $1,450 per month very comfortably covers the Peterson's apartment rental, pays for food and entertainment, and provides for supplemental health insurance and Medicare premiums. It covers charities, clothing, and cares for their modest new car. Even so, they will still save a tidy sum from each month's annuity income payment. Still saving new money becomes the name of the elderly game.

Before we settle on just one method or cite only one experience, let us learn a bit more about the specifics:

How Annuities Work

A given amount of invested money paid in to an annuity provides a given amount of monthly income beginning, for example, at age sixty-five and usually paid for life. A single premium annuity investment, which today averages about $13,750, will deliver at age sixty-five, or from any stated age after that, $100 or more per month, guaranteed for life or for a certain selected number of years, or for any combination of both. Annuity data is available from any life insurance company.

Annuities, designed to provide guaranteed income for life, are the reverse of life insurance. In life insurance you pay regular premiums to insure a lump sum settlement (or other option of payment) at death. With annuities, you can make a single purchase (or make annual payments) to insure regular monthly income for life. There are four basic annuity types:

1. *The straight life annuity* pays income to you for the rest of your life. It provides maximum income but stops at death, even if death occurs directly after payment is made.
2. *The life annuity with period certain* pays income for life, but for a guaranteed minimum period of time—five years, ten, or twenty years. If the annuitant dies within that period of time, the income is paid, for the rest of the time period, to the named beneficiary.

3. *The installment refund annuity* also pays an income for life. But if the annuitant dies before receiving as much money as he puts in, his beneficiary receives the difference.
4. *The joint-and-survivor annuity* provides for lifetime payments to two people. Its cost is based on the joint life expectancies of both payees.

There are single and joint life annuities:

Single life annuities:
  Costs: • dependent on age, sex, and size of contract
  Choices: • to be paid out for 0-years, 5-years, 10-years, or 20-years certain; either through installment or cash lump sum refunds if the annuitant dies before the years certain are up

Joint life annuities:
  Costs: • dependent on age, sex, and size of contract
  Choices: • to be paid out for 0-years, 5-years, 10-years, or 20-years certain; either through installment or cash lump sum refunds if the annuitant dies before the years certain are up
           • not reducing on first death
           • reducing on first death to 80 percent, to two-thirds, or to a lesser amount for a longer time
           • reducing only on death of spouse, not on primary insured's death

This examination is not a pitch for or against annuities. The basic facts are that this *is* a sound way to buy guaranteed income which you cannot outlive—income that starts being paid at a set date, usually age sixty-five. With life expectancy at age sixty-five being fifteen-plus years, there is a fair chance you will get more than your invested money back with no income worries to brood about.

There is more to the Peterson's old age security story. In addition to their monthly annuity income of $1,450, they will also be receiving an additional $575 per month since this is the combined total of the modest social security and pension benefit income they will continue to receive. Pile that $575 on top of the $1,450 annu-

ity and you get a total monthly income of $2,025. And, remember that they were already saving (about one-third) from the annuity payments alone.

Chet Peterson's parents' experience demonstrates that you can begin to "eat your own seed corn" if you program your appetite. The especially comforting new dimension to their story is the guaranteed income which comes forevermore from social security and pension benefit programs.

It is fair to recognize, however, that not everyone will be happy or comfortable with any plan that depends on the depletion of estate values—with no remainders and no inheritable leftovers.

In this specific zero estate case, the safest plan for the senior Petersons was the one worked out by a knowledgable life insurance professional, their son. He made the decision in behalf of his aging parents. It was his best plan for them. The children, in this case, expect to inherit nothing.

You and I are sharply aware that our lives are not this tidy and too often seem to be largely unmanageable; at best, life is frequently like a crap game. We buy fire insurance because we are betting that our house won't burn down. Then we rejoice if it doesn't, and we are comfortable in the assurance that we could get ourselves back under roof again if it did. We buy life insurance for protection. Then we hope that we will not die too soon, and that therefore, we will not need the protection. Later, we become aware that the passage of time has built up cash values which can then become part of our net worth as an accumulated asset.

Lay people are seldom very comfortable with insurance reasoning. We resent these costs, however necessary, but we insure because we are afraid not to. Even though actuaries and professional underwriters can make convincing cases from their experience data, we protest that we are insurance poor. Yet I'm sure you've never known a widow to complain about inheriting too much life insurance from her husband.

There is a reliable old axiom which says there are but two sources of income. Income either comes from man at work or from money at work. Today, we update this wisdom to person at work or property at work. All income comes from one of these sources.

Even though this chapter suggests and shows you "how to live it up—down to zero estate," many people will not demand such a fail-safe system as that represented by conservative lifetime annuities, which leave little or no remainder at death.

I ran into a real buzz-saw of contrary opinion while speaking on this subject, recently, at a conference of estate planning professionals. After I had cited the example of the Petersons, who had so tidily and securely managed their future with good help from their concerned children, bank trust people in the audience insisted that they had a much better method for "living it up." They made their points graphically and proved how they would safely manage estate assets for older clients, without coming to the end of the line, and also with no estate leftovers.

Given an estate residue of $200,000, they said they would prefer instead to prudently invest that money in double-A and triple-A quality bonds, with perhaps a most careful blend of selected utility stocks (depending on the client's own wishes and attitudes). They promptly demonstrated how that $200,000 could easily earn a safe return of between 7½ percent and 9½ percent which would provide approximately the same level of monthly and annual income as was paid to the Petersons from their annuity investment.

In this case, the estate planners and bank trust people assure the continuation of this income level for any number of years, and in the end you will get back all of your $200,000 besides. That surely would be "eating your cake and having it too."

Some savers and investors are not willing to go for bonds or even the most carefully selected utilities. Bonds have fixed values and are not inflation-proof, and utilities are dependent on economic and environmental factors for their dividend rates to rise and to appreciate in worth. Because of this dependency, utilities still may have a degree of value uncertainty. These investors have discovered compound interest, especially now with daily compounding. Banks and savings associations offer term savings certificates which are insured by the United States government up to $40,000 and beyond. Many investors own such insured maximum accounts, and have several at a number of different savings institutions. Interest rates vary but you can get as much as 7.75 percent, which, when compounded daily, delivers an 8.17 percent return. So there are choices, both in institutions and in savings methods, which pay reliably and well, and which are about as risk-free or risk-minimum as life ever can be.

In the estate planners' case under discussion, the $200,000 is to be invested at 8.17 percent and will earn $1,362 each month, to total $16,340 per year. This very nearly reaches the level of the annuity income example, *but* in addition, you retain all of your nest egg. Nothing is sacrificed from your consolidated "family fortune." To illustrate it graphically:

$200,000   entire principal invested, but it remains untouched and none is used

<u>× 8.17%</u>   daily compounded interest rate

$ 16,340   annual interest earned; this is $1,362 in monthly income—income for living

With the regular social security and pension benefits income, which can be conservatively estimated to total an extra $1,000 per month for another $12,000 per year, your monthly income totals reach $2,362 and your annual income would be $28,344. This ought to help immunize against inflation and health catastrophe. It should rather pleasantly help to finance the rest of our lives.

What about comparative risks between the annuity investment method and the bond-and-savings certificate route? Naturally, there are no absolute guarantees that protect in all circumstances. But there *are* governmental restrictions and controls on insurance offerings, and there is government insurance protection at work on savings certificate accounts. Each of these is conservative and prudent investing. In addition, at the double-A and triple-A bond levels, one is also into the highest safety zones available.

Finally, prudence should be a prime consideration in all investment. Careful, in-depth study and research should be done, and trusted, respected counsel should be sought. Advice beforehand, is so much more valuable than the most sympathetic understanding after things have gone wrong. There are investment account managers, and some savings organizations have agency account services available for clients. They keep the records, pay all taxes, and provide you with a regular accounting. They can buy or sell for your account, handle all transactions you agree upon, and send you a regular income check (interest, dividends, or combinations of both earnings and principal, as agreed upon between you). Their procedures are monitored by regulatory authorities, and their costs are not excessive.

On the other hand, there are other experienced and self-confident older persons who will protest against all this supervision and expensive account management, and perhaps rightly so. But it has been my observation that the fees of dedicated professionals most often save more than they cost. Check around among respected individual and corporate sources. Learn which advisers are most apt to become interested in you as persons, and in the earnings performance and safe conservation aspects of your financial affairs. Find the highest quality counsel you can, then relax and enjoy your life.

The specific case experiences portrayed here may be too neatly tied into $200,000 packages, as if that were the only estate size worth examining. You may say, with some justification, that people like that do not have a problem, and that "at those prices" who needs to fuss and worry. I am aware that even among middle- and upper-income people, not all are fat cats, and not all are graced with worry-free heaps of estate leftovers. We look now at several much more average cases; at people who are managing (or trying to cope) at generally lower levels, yet often in not dissimilar ways.

The reality to keep in mind is that any example is only that—one example. We must finally inject our own facts and figures, do our own calculations, so that we can read out our own conclusions.

Sophie Grimmer is a 70-year-old widow whose corporate executive husband left her only moderately well provided for financially, and even less well equipped with the knowledge and skill to cope with the new experience of handling her own finances. This practical widow sought reliable banking counsel and her $85,000 estate is now at work earning what it safely can, with all of the details managed by bank trust people whom she knows and respects. Each month they pay out any income her invested residue has earned, and each year—especially those in which she has specific goals, such as a trip, an important purchase, or a gift she *wishes to make—her advisers help her dip moderately into principal in order to finance these extras.*

Before we feel too sorry for Sophie Grimmer and her limited monthly income from her invested funds—which totals between $500 and $600—take note that she is a widow who happens to be additionally blessed with her spouse's share of her husband's social security and with his pension fund income. In this case, these happen to be quite generous. Sophie gets about $933 each month from these sources. And this, added to her asset earnings, raises her monthly income to $1,500 per month. And remember, all this came from what is really a modest estate balance.

There are so many ways, so many sensible reasons, to go right on living—to enjoy "living it up."

An older couple by the name of Winston were talking with a son and daughter-in-law about such matters as these we are examining here. The senior Winston mused aloud that it would be nice if they didn't have to use up all of their assets before both parents died so that they could leave some leftovers for the son and his wife.

Everyone nodded pleasantly, and after a time the son said:

"That would be wonderful, Dad, if in the end you do have some unspent assets to pass on to us. We always wanted to take a leisurely trip to Greece and that's exactly what we will do when we get that inheritance."

Winston senior blinked a bit, and looked quizzically at his wife for just a moment, and then he said:

"Mother, tomorrow let's go down to that travel agency we usually go to for trips we're planning. I want them to start working on just such a leisurely trip to Greece—just for you and me."

Here is a similar experience to share. Ray Albrecht told about the extra fancy cruise his wife Alice signed them up for last winter:

"Alice bought us this real swell cruise—it surely was one grand boat ride, I'll tell you. And you know, Alice is paying for it all, herself. She decided this would be a good idea, and that she was willing to take a slightly smaller inheritance when I cash in my chips."

In the end, so many of our deepest concerns turn out to be academic exercises anyway. Take Cousin Charley in quite a different case:

> *Charley is not one of those soured souls who always attacks each day, re-celebrating each new slice of bad luck, kicking, complaining and cussing. Not Charley, for he had a happier view of things. When he ended up alone, he moved into the county home in his community. It was a remarkably pleasant place, nestled gently into the side of a rolling hill, with trees and gardens all around, and with kindly care from dedicated professionals who served with love the hundred or more older persons for whom this was now "their last home."*
>
> *But even as a county home, this public facility cost him almost $600 per month. Charley's money ran out—but he licked that problem, in time. Now he lives in that same cheery room in that pleasant hillside home. He receives the same kindly care, the same good food, and all of the medication he always got to keep him alive and not too unhappy. The only thing that changed was that now the county pays for Charley's care, and he winks as he acknowledges that he "paid his dues all these years." Now it is his turn to accept, and not to knock, the welfare machine he lives on. Charley had inadvertently lived it up—down to the zero point of his estate.*

Where do you stand in your own planning, and what are your own dollars-and-cents feelings about retired and later life? Are you the kind of person or family who could consider cashing in all of your chips? Could you, for example, invest your own lump sum total in an annuity for your lifetime; or are you more comfortable with an alternate choice, such as putting your bundle into safe and sound certificates or into highest quality bonds? What is your answer to that investment credo which asks: "Would you rather eat well or sleep well for the rest of your lifetime?" Assets may be dandy, but income is even dandier.

For many of us thoughtful and sensible persons, the entire exercise and discussion of how to get rid of money and how to use up our own estate, is either purely academic or irrelevant. Either we believe we are too young for this to concern us, or we may be so old and so set in our conserving ways, that we cannot bring ourselves to even listen with an open mind. But there are two realities which bear on these views. If we remain rigid about relaxing in our later life, grasping everything tightly to our nervous bosoms, someone else will get to spend it and enjoy it in our stead. And if we are younger, there are things we can do well in advance to enhance our later choices and our own future prospects. If you don't send your security ahead, it won't be there. One step in that direction is to learn a bit more about the magic of compound interest.

Savings certificates and E and H Savings Bonds are often overlooked as investments. By the time many of us learn the secret of compound interest, it is too late to do much to correct our neglect, and we end up with too little to compound.

Savings association authorities outline a sample plan: To illustrate, if you begin at age 50 (although you may start anytime you like), and invest $100 per month for fifteen years, you will be able to draw out, beginning at age 65, $100 per month for as long as you live. And in the end, your heirs will get back more than you invested in those fifteen years.

Obviously, you can alter the amount invested per month, and your end result will reflect the larger or smaller amounts paid in. If your appetite or your expectation of need, for example, is for extra income for life of $500 per month beginning at age 65, then you could begin at age 50 to put $500 per month into this type of savings account.

Savings experts say further, that if you had invested a similar amount in an I.R.A., that is an Individual Retirement Account (or in a Keogh Plan if you are self-employed), you might have tripled your money rather than just doubling it. The difference lies in the untaxed dollars which you put into an I.R.A. (or a Keogh Plan), which provide extra investable savings which would also be compounding. Compound interest and the newer daily compounding, which computer technology has made possible, are now facts of life. Time is all that is required for them to function at maximum return levels.

No wonder Baron de Rothschild is reputed to have called compound interest the eighth wonder of the world. It is pure magic, and through it, say financial advisers, almost anyone could become rich.

2

Where Income Keeps Coming From

Good as it is to inherit a library–or anything else of worthy value–it is far better to collect one.
ANON.

One of the best kept secrets, and also one of the most comforting for persons who are growing older, is the delightful fact that there will continue to be a variety of new income sources which will bring new hope into our lives.

Guaranteed income is the first of these; optional income is still another very promising source of new money for our later years; and, of course, asset income is the final crown on all of our lifetime of saving and struggling—to assure that we should not end up living in old age want.

People who are older—those approaching retirement or those already retired—have a lot of very real concerns about how they will be able to cope with the high cost of growing older. There is hope, and part of it is in the form of additional new income.

Guaranteed Income

The principal components of guaranteed income are social security and pensions. For some there are also life insurance annuities.

14

Life Expectancy

Life expectancy is the controlling factor in determining how much you will ultimately receive in guaranteed income. How long do you expect to live; what age are you now; what age will you be when you retire? (Remember that retirement may come earlier than you now expect.) What do the life expectancy tables indicate to you in extra years of life after age sixty-two; after age sixty-five? In addition, each individual should consider how many years of life were granted to parents and grandparents, since inherited factors control longevity to a large degree. Once you assemble these factors into a picture, think of life expectancy as so many months and years of continuing new income from guaranteed income sources. (For planning purposes, couples might average together their years of life expectancy.)

At age sixty-two, spouses on average have close to eighteen years left to live. At age sixty-five, the average life expectancy for a couple is about seventeen years. Remember, these are averages: women should add and men subtract a few years, based on the tables of statistics. During this time budgets remain, and bills for living expenses have a way of showing up regularly month after month. This tells us that we had better have dependable income for each month and each remaining year.

To project ahead and to understand, with reasonable accuracy, what our own guaranteed income expectation will be, we need to undertake an exercise or two. If we multiply our age–sixty-two life expectancy of eighteen years by twelve months, we get 216 monthly income occasions or 216 units of income we should count on. If you are opting for retirement benefits beginning at age sixty-five, you should multiply seventeen years by twelve months which will add up to 204 monthly units of income. These 200-plus monthly occasions are the number of times you should expect guaranteed income to arrive. It is also the number of times bills will appear. To make the example graphic:

Age 62:

18	years of life expectancy
× 12	months per year of income expected (and needed)
216	monthly units of income expectation

Age 65:

```
 17    years of life expectancy
× 12    months per year of income expected (and needed)
────
204    monthly units of income expectation
```

For purposes of further examining this illustration in terms of specifics, we will use only the conservatively rounded-off figure of 200 expected monthly income units. Where will this income come from, and how much will it add up to?

Social Security Benefits

Social security, for most of us who are in middle- and upper-income brackets, will be based upon or very close to paid-in maximums. *Even though times keep changing and inflation keeps rising, cost-of-living increases or adjustments are indexed into social security, and payments are being increased periodically.* For this demonstration we are using the conservative figure of $700 per month of social security income which will come regularly to each eligible couple (single individuals should expect about two-thirds of this amount).

If you are projecting these monthly amounts from age sixty-two, social security advises that you can expect to receive about 20 percent less (or abut $560 monthly), with these percentages increasing about 5 percent per year for every year until age sixty-five. Let us take a look now at the total lifetime social security income expectation according to your life expectancy at age sixty-five.

Age 65:

```
 $700    expected monthly social security income
× 200    monthly units of expected income
────────
$140,000
```

This is the amount of social security income you can expect if you are a sixty-five-year-old couple, and it will keep coming during the 200 months of your life expectancy. (Changing factors may vary these amounts, but nothing can alter the accuracy of this concept.) Wives who paid into their own social security funds can expect their social security share to raise these figures.

To personally tailor this data to your own situation, list in the space provided the social security income you have been advised that you will be receiving. Social security offices near you can project approximately how much you can expect to receive in monthly payments.

Age 65:

$_____   monthly social security you can expect

   × 200   monthly income units you can expect

$_____   this is the total projected amount of social security income you can expect to receive.

Pension Benefits

There should be comfort in these facts, but this is only the beginning of the good news. To the reality of social security income, we now add still another guaranteed income source—your pension benefit income. If you should happen to be among those relative few who are still not covered by a pension program where you work, you can build your own by starting a Keogh Plan if you are self-employed, or through an Individual Retirement Account (I.R.A.).

Pension payments, on a national average, can be expected to average $500 per month. This is especially true since the new pension law (ERISA) was signed in 1974.

If your pension is scheduled to be higher, bless you for your good fortune in having chosen your employment situation so providentially. If you expect a pension of less than $500 per month, you may still be able to do some things to augment your pension income. Your spouse may be able to set up his or her own I.R.A. plan or other program. You should lose no time in finding out from a reliable, expert authority if any pension alternatives make sense in your situation, especially if you wish to boost what will be coming to you. Another example:

Age 65

$500   expected pension benefit income

× 200   monthly units of expected pension income

$100,000

This is the amount of pension benefit income you can expect (now vested and guaranteed in your name) if you are a qualifying or a sixty-five year-old retiree. This amount will continue to arrive year after year during the 200 months of your projected life expectancy. Obviously, this is but one example. Be assured, however, that there is a pension in your future even if you have to set up your own.

Were you even remotely aware of the size of the pension trust which has been firmly established in your name? Future improvements will tighten still further the secure hold you have on pension rights, for there will be insured funding, and vesting will follow mobile individuals in job-change situations. The point is that we can now relax a lot better about pension income expectations.

It will help if you personalize this example by listing in the spaces provided the pension benefit income you have been advised that you will be receiving. Be sure that you promptly check with personnel or pension benefit managers where you are employed to determine as exactly as possible just what you can expect to be receiving in pension income.

Age 65:

$_____ monthly pension income you can expect
× 200   monthly income units of expected pension income

$_____ this is the total of projected pension benefit
          income you can expect to receive. It is the corpus
          of your pension trust fund.

Finally, space has been provided for you to figure the total of your social security benefits added to your pension benefits, both of which you have now factored from the figures of your own earnings and vesting.

$_____ your total social security trust fund
$_____ your total pension income trust fund

$_____ Combined total of your personal and family
          guaranteed income funds set up in your name,
          which you can expect to draw on for the 200

months (more or less) of your own life expectancies.

Since bills and budgets are usually monthly occurrences, you should convert these figures to monthly income.

$_____ your projected monthly social security income totals

$_____ your projected monthly pension income

$_____ your total projected monthly income from these basic guaranteed income sources

Some may consider it unnecessary, and even irrelevant, to project the amounts of these two income sources according to our life expectancy, or to show these as accumulated trust fund corpora. Life and these social systems are all too difficult to predict. That is true, but the exercise does encourage our own planning; it helps to know specifically about such guaranteed income. Person at work or property at work—a good axiom to remember.

The foregoing assured income sources are real because you, as a person at work during your earning years, had money deducted from earnings to which matching monies were added (for social security); and similarly, still more money (pension benefits) were set aside in your name. This money is really part of a deferred income which is tax-free until paid out. In both of these funds, the monies became property at work. Their combined corpora are assets set aside in your name, just as are ownership in real estate, stocks, or bonds. You own the former just as rightfully as you own the latter. There is actually less risk with these assets and their obligation to pay you regularly than there is in any other investment or savings categories.

What About the Security of Social Security?

Social security funds are adequate and secure—and Congress and the President have recently assured their security until well past the year 2000. Further, be assured that the system will be additionally funded, if and when that might become necessary, from other sources of taxation. It will be done because social security must be kept sound.

The same doubts may be expressed about the security of pension funds, since in years past some did turn up with big promises and little payout. However, under the Employee Retirement Income Act (ERISA) of 1974, more stringent controls on pension safety have been built in, and more protection will be added as needed. For our purposes in this study, it is both realistic and sensible to live with positive expectations. Pensions are a reliable cushion!

Optional Income

Optional income is income over which you can exercise control, and which results from choices you make. It is income available from the conversion of existing assets, such as mini-career jobs; hobbies turned into small businesses, and insurance policies. The list is long and the ideas abundant.

Life Insurance Values

Two-thirds of American families are insured and they own cash values that have accrued on their policies, and that are part of net worth assets. You may feel that you cannot use up your life insurance because you have been taught that it is an almost sacred convenant for protection. That may be true, but only to a point. After your need for essential protection has passed—children grown and gone, mortgages largely retired—when you are older and have other protective income options, you may have less need for emergency money.

Independent insurance consultants and investment advisory professionals are suggesting more and more often that older persons (those already retired or close to it), take a practical look at the accumulated cash values they own in their life insurance. Since these values are really your property, they can be borrowed against at low rates. Depending upon whether protection needs are adequately covered, cash values can be converted into annuities for extra retirement income. They can be borrowed against or cashed in, and that money may then be put to other earning work.

The Life Insurance Fact Book, published annually by the American Council of Life Insurance, reports that insured persons and families own an average of approximately $40,000* of life insurance. It is

* 1978 data

theirs to do with as they please. If your need now is more for income and less for protection, then that is an avenue you should explore, as long as you seek competent and trusted advice, and as long as you do not tamper with protection values you might need later. It is well in these considerations to stay straight on "which is the horse and which is the rider," on what are your needs and wishes. If you own the national life insurance average of $40,000, and if three-fourths is in cash values by this time, by cashing in or borrowing against your insurance now you can pick up extra income for living (as much as $200 per month at the safest 8 percent bond or savings certificate you can find.) You should decide—after careful consideration and advice.

Home Ownership Values

Individual and family-owned homes are another vital asset, with two thirds of the population owning their own homes. (This proportion is higher in rural and non-metropolitan areas, and lower in strictly urban centers.) These same homes are 85 percent paid for by the time their owners retire. They are another marketable, or convertible asset, one on which you can borrow at any time. And, homes are one asset that seem to keep appreciating in value as well.

You may not think that this is the best time of your life to put your house in hock—and it may not be—but, at the same time, it does seem ironic to witness older persons who go hungry or live in worry and in actual want while occupying such a valued asset as a home. You can't "eat your house" but if you get hungry enough, figuratively speaking, selling your home or borrowing against its values (especially at a sufficiently late age) might be just the ticket you need to help you relax during your remaining days.

A National Association of Realtors bulletin reports that existing homes have recently been selling at an average of approximately $50,000*, and that this trend is rapidly accelerating upward. (New homes are averaging near $60,000* in cost.) Also, owners are troubled by increasing real estate taxes; they are high and going higher. But what are the smart alternatives? There are more apartment rental opportunities available, but their rates are climbing, too, reflecting the same cost increases that homeowners are themselves so keenly aware

* 1978 data

of. In sum for the purposes of this examination, your paid-for home (or one nearly paid-for) is an asset—an asset to provide you with suitable housing, to cash in by selling, or to borrow against if immediate cash is your first urgent need.

If your home were sold at the national average price at present, you would own sufficient capital to earn an extra $400 per month (at 8 percent). You would no longer own that asset; you would have left behind that "shelter to windward" we all seem to take solace from. But you would have been absolved from higher real estate taxes and higher maintenance costs (including today's new security consideration). You would have the money to invest in new, simpler housing, if that is your wish. Or, you would have that substantial sum of money to invest for earning new income to live on. This income could, in part, pay your monthly rental now, and also provide some monthly income from the investment of the remainder. All we are studying here are the choices available to us.

While not every family unit or person ought to cut loose from familiar neighborhoods and friends, the conversion of home assets to income production will fit in at some time of life, with the aims of those who are bent on simplifying their lives.

A fresh word may be in order on mounting real estate taxes, which are soaring in most areas. Perhaps we need wiser bankers (and there are an increasing number) or we may, ourselves, have to change our sacred view of property. We may be coming to a time and circumstance, especially at this point in our changing lives, when it makes sense to refinance our homes to provide ready cash to pay for rising taxes, higher heating bills, and other home-related burdens that we are not now able to cope well with. It may be a startling idea, but it is being done by some very prudent and conservative people.

For example, if you have the audacity to take a brand new, late in life mortgage for $20,000 against your mean-average $50,000 home, for the next fifteen years of your life, you would have ready money to meet home-operating and living expenses. The appreciation in your home's new value would more than outdistance the interest you would pay. And, you would still own your asset.

Velma Freedland did just that—at age seventy-four. She convinced her very conservative banker to give her the loan she needed to fix up and maintain her lovely little home. And she got that new mortgage for thirty years. A thirty-year mortgage at age seventy-four. Even the banker smiles, a touch nervously perhaps. But he is aware, as Velma is, that the increase in values and her limited life expectancy will, in the end, leave more than enough to pay off the "senior citizen" mortgage which Velma is using. She is actually using her home to remove the cares and concerns of rising housing costs. That home is serving her in the very best, most sensible way, rather than remaining a static asset to be left for someone else. Who needs those values, that assets-converted-to-cash-power, more than Velma?

Homes account on a national average, for upwards of 50 percent of most families' total net worth. Therefore, it is easy to understand why we take such secure comfort from home ownership. We see our home as an anchor against much of life's uncertainty.

Reverse Mortgage Bulletin

During the development of this concept to enable older persons to use their "house-power" to help finance home taxes, maintenance, and increased living expenses, our research was also turning up a very similar practice long popular in France. The use of home equity to finance home retention, and to improve the chance for senior citizens to stay in their familiar home circumstance, is being variously called *split equity, reverse annuity,* or simply reverse mortgage. It is only now being seriously considered, and attempted, in this country.

Without being familiar with all of the technicialities, Velma Freedland has been applying this self-same principle. Simply stated, the *reverse annuity mortgage* enables an older couple to borrow a fixed amount of money based on the value of the home property. The borrower does not have to repay the loan; it would remain as a lien against the estate when the person dies; the loan would be in the form of monthly payments. This plan alleviates two major problems of many older persons—a lack of sufficient money for everyday needs, and the fear of losing their home—plus, of course, softening tax burdens.

Reverse mortgages are just that: Savings and loan groups, banks, or other home loan lenders would pay the borrower, in monthly income installments, a sum based on a percentage (probably 80 percent) of the property's value. The lender recovers the loan when the home is sold or when the owner dies.

There is a happy justice in the promise which enables the retired older citizen to put the equity in his home to work providing needed, and comforting, retirement income. In effect, he is taking out a series of monthly loans by using his home as collateral.

Some of the more conservative may get nervous about such "risk of hearth and home," and about running up new mortgage obligations at this late stage in life. But even here there is hope. With homes appreciating over the last five years at the rate of approximately 14 percent per year, even the reverse-annuity-mortgaged family home of older persons should, in the end, be worth even more than any encumbrance levied against it.

If it is your need or wish, there is another rather obvious source for acquiring extra new income after your job-career activity and their income have stopped delivering paychecks. That is the new career activity which is increasingly available and attractive for greater numbers of people. This is especially true of those who may be retiring early—whether to get into something new or pushed out by the company. Often these jobs can be part-time, with flexible hours, jobs through which we can get acquainted with a new area, meet new people, and find new fields to conquer.

If you are still resisting the idea and feel that optional income is "maybe money," that it is not a part of your life's realities, keep the faith a bit longer. A series of opportunities is forming for earning a little new leisure money from second or third careers, and from part-time work that we may enjoy as much as we did our old jobs. There is a glow of confidence in any post-career job activity that comes from picking up some new money in some new way. Besides, this can take the pressure off of our budgets.

There are those who demur, however, like my new friend whom I call "Doubting Thomas," who turned up in the front row at one of the seminars I was conducting on this subject. He objected to most of the encouraging and positive ideas I paraded past him, seeming determined to puncture more possibility balloons that he was willing to breathe new air into.

*"If you want me to work after I am retired, then why should I
even bother to retire; why not just keep on working at my old
job?"*

My view then and now is that this is fine—stay on your old job
if you want to; stay if you can; stay if they will permit you to keep
working, and earning, after their mandatory retirement age. I
have observed that everyone retires sometime. Even if he owns the
place, people want him out. Very few of us—mostly
professionals—have the option of staying after the retirement age
or of phasing down gradually. It does not fit into the system. Even
"Doubting Thomas" will be retired, sometime, and there are
ideas here to keep him happily active, if he wants such activity,
and if he seeks some new income. I also witness that mini-career
jobs and the income they produce can most often be enjoyed with
less pressure, with fewer deadlines, and with less risk to ourselves, if the job ultimately ends.

Retirement and the years of our aging can be the problem we may
have feared; or it can be a fresh new opportunity, often beyond any we
have imagined. The people who seem to get the most fun and the most
delightful benefits from the creative use of this new freer time of life,
are the ones who still yearn to grab the brass ring, to experience one
more fast turn around life's track. They are the most fulfilled, satisfied, and exciting folks to be near. Whatever your extra-career goal, if
you have or want one, you will be delighted to find an extra offering
of fresh, optional income. Why not consider trying it—at least for a
while, and for a few extra dollars?

To stimulate your thinking about potential new income sources
available to you, take a look at the following list of some of the more
obvious possibilities for finding new money, for discovering unexpected new income for your later years:

Potential Sources of New Income or Asset Conversion:

A. DEFERRED CAREER INCOME:
>   stock options, severance settlements.

B. PROFIT-SHARING INCOME:
>   scheduled payout or lump-sum settlements; dispersal money
>   from credit unions; other group-funded retirement trusts.

C. OTHER ESTABLISHED TRUSTS:
   family, corporate, or organizational trusts; dispersal or income.

D. NEW INHERITANCE:
   expected legacies or surprises, often from remote, and unexpected sources.

E. ESTATE SETTLEMENTS:
   including cash residues; with real estate and personal property; gifts, heirlooms, equities.

F. BUY-AND-SELL AGREEMENTS:
   scheduled payout or lump-sum settlements from ownership changes; dispersal of owned shares.

G. PROPERTY SALES SETTLEMENTS:
   distribution of shares, or cashed-in values, from real property, buildings, land, other property.

H. ASSET INCOME:
   interest earned, and dividends received; coupons maturing; interest, new shares or scheduled payout from mutual or other funds; interest and principal payments from notes, mortgages, other obligations, including appreciated values.

I. RENTAL PAYMENTS:
   from farm properties; family homes still retained; other real estate or business properties, whether wholly owned or shared with other family members; rents realized from co-ops, apartments, cottages, or condominiums, in off-seasons.

J. FEES STILL EARNED OR RECEIVED:
   contractual or deferred payments, fees still earned whether due from past or present advisory or consulting arrangements.

K. LIFE INSURANCE SETTLEMENTS:
   endowment payouts, other varying options; cash values left with insurers whick keep producing interest or dividends; other maturing coverage to be paid out according to schedules set; plus cash settlements at insured's death.

L. ANNUITY PAYMENTS:
   regular paid-up annuities; new single premium annuities purchased for retirement; variable and zero estate annuity income.

M. ROYALTIES, PATENTS, LICENSE INCOME:
   income from assigned or leased rights, from sales of patented
   products assigned, and from creative properties.

N. COMMISSIONS:
   new commissions still being earned, or still due on previous
   efforts or from former contracts; and from deferred arrangements from former connections.

O. CASH APPRECIATION:
   growth resulting from aging antiquities; from new buying and
   selling; from sales of collections, art works, books, coins,
   stamps, glassware, furniture and from other collectibles or
   possessions.

P. TAX SHELTERED PROPERTY:
   systematic selling-off of ownership rights of lands, conces-
   sions, inventories, shared, oil and mineral rights, real property; any other tax sheltered income or selling assets.

Q. PENSION PAYMENTS:
   scheduled payout of Keogh Plans, I.R.A., or corporate or
   other organizational pension programs; either the income pro-
   duced, or payout of principal.

R. HEALTH PROTECTION POLICIES:
   not Medicare supplementals, but those which pay out in extra
   cash, or which pay out cash over and above medical or hospital expenses.

S. SOCIAL SECURITY BENEFITS:
   individual or couple benefits upon age qualification; special
   disability payments, or death settlements. (Cost-of-living increases are indexed in, usually annually.)

T. SUPPLEMENTAL SECURITY INCOME:
   for those who can qualify due to diminished income and lim-

ited net worth; a supplemental aid to those who fall below dignity living levels.

U. NEW EARNED INCOME:
any new mini-career or even substantial new enterprise; jobs or services which earn because of singular expertise; hobbies earning income; creative works which are sold; avocational activity which produces income.

V. DISABILITY PAYMENTS:
governmental, civil service, military-connected benefit payments or settlements.

W. SPECIAL, EXTRA PENSIONS:
railroad brotherhood, teacher, civil service, plus other earned rights additional to normal lay career pensions; benefits and rights acquired long ago, early in forgotten careers—now due to pay out.

X. DEBT OBLIGATIONS:
short or long term debt obligations due you; alimony, support payments; repayment of promisary obligations; and settlements still due you.

Y. GIFTS, LEGACIES, AWARDS:
for favors granted, for love given and exchanged; for no greater reason than that one of these arrives to surprise you.

Z. ENJOYMENT OF PRINCIPAL:
any owned assets which are turned into cash and drawn-down either as income or in lump sum; sales of homes, equities, any other property which will now begin to be used up.

&. WHO CAN TELL—WHAT ELSE?
No list like this can possibly include or anticipate all new income surprises.

Naturally, not all of the foregoing list of income expectations fit all families or individuals, but it is appropriate to check into any new and even surprising possibility which might help in your planning.

It might be a profitable and enjoyable exercise to dream over reminders of such varieties of potential good fortune—most of which we may say will only happen to others. None of this is worth a fig if it does not fit our own realities. What, then, are the hard facts of our own experience. Which of these, or other potentials, could still fit into our lives?

As a meaningful exercise, why not now fill in your own checklist, your own new income expectations inventory. Use the general list as an inspiration and apply any that are probable to your own chart.

Guaranteed Income Sources:	Annual Amounts:
Social security	$ _____
Supplemental security income	_____
Pension benefits	_____
Profit-sharing income	_____
Annuity income	_____
Deferred career income	_____
Retired career benefits (teacher, civil service, etc.)	_____
Disability payments	_____

Optional Income Sources:	Annual Amounts:
New part- or full-time career	$ _____
Selling collectibles	_____
Other	_____
	_____

Asset Income Sources:	Annual Amounts:
Interest expected	$ _____
	_____
Dividends expected	_____
	_____
Other	_____
	_____
	_____

Is it possible that you may still be convinced that you will never again earn another new dollar? In spite of all this evidence and promise to the contrary, are you still worrying, "What if our money runs out before we do?"

Asset Income

Despite the foregoing charts and checklists, you will admit that we have not until now been persuading you that you are really rich. I have not been peeking into your private pockets nor have I been prying around in your safety deposit boxes and safes. But the word is that most of us have been saving money in recent times at a fantastic rate. Accountants and taxing authorities call these *assets,* and what they earn is called *asset income.* Most of us have been living scared, we have been saving carefully in these uncertain days of economic instability. National data shows that we have been squirreling away very tidy sums of saved, and invested capital. We have been fattening up our security mattresses. In fact, we have become so good at holding on, and so slow at letting go, that our asset income power is starting—in many, many cases—to match our guaranteed and our optional income power.

All this may not be the best for our national economy, but it is very good for our retirement economy. It allows us to feel good about living it up a little, to really enjoy the rewards of these available choices, for the rest of our later years. Why not let them be more golden?

It makes sense to pause just a moment in all of this heady excitement about this too often unappreciated new income, to take a thoughtful look into our overall financial condition. What do we, as an individual or as a family unit, add up to in net worth assets? This has particular significance at this juncture because we have been so busy celebrating how fat our monthly cash flow is going to be—and we may suddenly awaken to other, sterner realities. And yet, we can become aware that these guaranteed incomes promise to take some pressure off of some of our needs and compulsions to save, save, save.

3

Coping With the Cost of Growing Older

*Man makes plans; and then he makes more plans
. . . and nothing ever works. But it is still laud-
able for Man to go on making plans.*
                              paraphrased from The
                              Threepenny Opera by
                              BERTOLT BRECHT

If we cannot hide from inflation, then what are our constructive alternatives? The steady rise in the cost of goods and services, and the steady decline in the purchasing power of our money, is
an inexorable trend which marches unevenly upward throughout economic history (not only in our country but just about anywhere else in
this world where we might be satisfied to live). And what are we, as
worried and frustrated individuals, able to do about it?

There are some options still open and ready to work in our behalf.
For example, at least from this time forward, most of our income
sources are increasingly benefiting from indexing, built-in cost-of-living adjustments. Most, though not all, to be sure! This blessed new
upward indexing feature helps give us hope as we try to keep in some
kind of lock-step pace with the cost of our living. The solution, or our
accommodation to inflation's reality, is not in worrying about it in
helpless despair, but is in how well we plan to out-race and out-dis-
tance it.

You become acutely aware—from an asset and liability exercise
like the foregoing. You can see just where you stand, right now and in

the long term—of the economic order—or lack of it—in your daily lives and for your aging years. You are probably also made a bit more comfortably aware that you are better off than had been your suspicion. That you may, indeed, be able to really live—for as long as you live. As individuals, we will do better if we take specific steps to keep pace with inflation, to rise with it as much as possible. The question which haunts us most is not just the vague idea of inflation, but rather, how much is it costing us in net loss slippage? How much are we slipping back in the purchasing power of our money.

It is sadly true that inflation does exist, and that it is invasive in our economic lives. But, it is also true—at the same time—that fresh factors are at work to help take some of the sting out of inflation.

Inflation is again rising, and once before it reached the intolerable high of 12 percent. However, the recent eight-year average stands at 6.25 percent. Not comfortable, but not catastrophic when you consider how much of your retirement income from social security, pensions and dividends, is indexed to keep at least partly in step with such inflation.

The other, even greater, supportive reality is that appreciation in the worth of real estate and other non-fixed property values also helps wonderfully to keep us from falling too far behind in net loss slippage from inflation's bite.

Take some solace from the fact that there is little or no real netloss slippage for anyone who receives social security or other indexed pension benefit payments or for anyone who also owns real estate (including the home they live in). True, we must still fight to keep inflation under better control, but those who also own assets which earn and grow are just that much better off. They are keeping up since the assets are growing in some kind of near-even pace with inflation's rise. Not perfect, but not catastrophically terminal either. As Thomas Collins, a noted retirement writer, said in his syndicated column, "Any retired person sitting in his or her own debt-free home gets a little richer every night because home and land prices keep going up."

Our own best answer lies in eliminating, or at least minimizing, what inflation's net-loss slippage will be. Not what the rate is nationally or internationally, but the difference between that rate of rise and how our assets and income rise through indexing or through appreciation. For it is true that our incomes will inch upward, and our assets will grow in their worth, even though inflation's leeching effect fuels part of that rise. This new way of looking at things is real enough and I, therefore, grow weary as we read in the daily press, and as we hear the dirge and din of the nervous TV newscasts, about double-digit inflation. Inflation is a real and worldwide threat. But, although you and I cannot lick that all by ourselves, we can keep our wits focused not on *inflation screaming* but on the *slippage of our net loss,* and what final effect that has on our situation. How much are we falling behind in net dollars and in net purchasing power, if we are falling behind at all?

Happily, you will discover when you reach the end of your career, that it costs less to live in the years of your retirement, much less than when you were still success-bent. Sylvia Porter reports in her column that it costs a third less, and a wide spectrum of retiree experience bears that out. You will be able to get by on two-thirds of the income you needed when one or both of you were still working full time.

While retirement income is covered in more specific detail in other parts of this book, suffice it to say that most of us will be taking in more in after-work income in our later years than we now expect. Our assets appreciate annually; we ride upward with part of the rise of inflation; and most of us, whether we admit it or even know it rationally, are going to be worth much more than we now believe.

It is true, however, that investing, especially in our later years, can be troublesome. We should seek the highest earnings and the highest payout to give us maximum income, but we should also avoid risking the safety of our asset principal.

There are variable investment strategies: variable equities and mutual funds which mix part growth stocks with part fixed high-yielding investments such as bonds, there are variable annuities, and for those who can truly afford the risk, there are still growth stock situations. There is also real estate investing for those who have the skill and the stomach for that appreciating asset. It is a category which has been trading ever upward, and which relies on the rampaging cost of replacement labor and materials, while it climbs even higher on the shortage factor of improved residential and commercial land and on other real estate property. There is profit growth in real estate; and there is also a strong inflation immunity in home ownership. But, we never know for how long.

Greed, in later years investing, is risky and foolish. "Pigs," it is said in business school parlance, "are slaughtered in the market." Prudent judgment and investing always make sense. It comes down to whether we want to eat better or sleep better. Mixed portfolios, help keep the inflation-proofing growth factor alive and at work. They also make quite sure that there will be income—a sufficient retirement income—to make the soundest sense for most of us. As we toy with the idea of growing older, we should not trifle with income—it is the sweetest music in retirement.

Finally, after we have innoculated our situations as well as we sensibly can, how about settling down into some kind of economic serenity; reminding ourselves that we are, after all, still alive and still pretty well off, all things considered? The truth is that most of us have grown mighty talented, after years of careful concern and tight-fisted managing, at worrying as much out of habit as out of any real necessity. We cannot imagine being happy with *less* and we always seem to be wanting *more*. I do not suggest that this is wrong, though it may be unrealistic. *More* is not always better, nor is it forever possible—or even necessary.

As if speeded-up inflation levels pecking away at our pocketbooks and our psyches were not enough, we are now also staring out ahead at the chilling threat of health care and the cost of health catastrophe. We become acutely aware, as we keep adding more and more to our stretching life span, and especially as we remain alive and alert longer, that everyone is living with the threat of some terminal illness. Death, after all, is the ultimate in terminal illnesses.

We may watch others malinger, and pray that when it is our turn we will go quickly. But we have only limited and usually unacceptable choices in this matter. It is costly to be ill, and it will cost plenty to be laid up—with or without third-party payers, with or without government help or extra insurance assistance. And it will continue to cost more and more because today we enjoy the life-mending and life-extending benefits of highly trained special skills and experience, and the dedicated professionals who operate the equipment and employ fresh techniques of such wondrous, and costly, sophistication. They serve the ill and infirm seven days and nights each week, bringing both comfort and healing. And it all does cost a very large bundle of money, indeed.

A news bulletin of the American Association for Retired Persons quotes from a report on "Nursing Home Care in the United States: Failure in Public Policy," which was prepared by a special senate subcommittee: "About $2 of every $3 in nursing revenue is publicly financed, with Medicaid paying about 60 percent of the nation's $3.7 billion nursing home bill and Medicare paying another 7 percent."

Recent Health-Care Cost Examples

- Heart blockage by-pass operation with high blood pressure complications
  Employment group plus supplemental paid all but about $150. $13,500

- Heart attack; heart blockage by-pass operation; pacemaker installed.
  Medicare plus Medicare Extended paid for all of it. $30,000 plus

- Complicated heart, blood, and circulation problems; heart-artery by-passes; plus months of complications.
  Employment group plus supplemental coverage paid essentially all of it. $44,000 plus

- Uncomplicated major surgery for hernia repair.
  Medicare plus Medicare Extended paid for all costs. $ 1,600

- Toe operation (neuroma); not serious.
  Medicare plus Medicare Extended paid for all but a few minor charges (approximately $50). $ 900

The point of these current examples is less to reassure about how well everything was covered—though that, too, is significant—but rather to make the point that these varied cases, even those of substantial cost, were being covered, that they can be covered, and that it is possible to cope with this cost of growing older.

While we are at it, we should recognize and bless Medicare, whatever its costs and inadequacies. This is a view I bring from a long experience as a hospital trustee, as well as a not-infrequent patient with my own personal health problems. We can, indeed, respect Medicare as a very large and protective health-care umbrella, for it is just that. Think where we would be in our older years without its protection. But, Medicare can only be part of the answer; its coverage can only "shock-proof" us, we probably couldn't afford the high total cost of blanket coverage for every ache and pain. Medicare is, after all, just a part of our financial coping machinery.

Beyond Medicare, there is much we must do for ourselves. I put more emphasis on buying extra risk protection than on saving and hoarding against unseen and uncertain "rainy days" which may never come, or may not, in our case, be totally catastrophic. We will feel a lot safer, and rest a lot more serenely, if we know that we have adequate health-care protection, and that unexpected costs are borne by third-party payers, that is, the supplemental coverage which serves to shore up the leaks, to plug up any gaps of Medicare coverage so essential to our later years.

For those of you who are as yet not covered under Medicare, I suggest a careful review of how much of your employment coverage you will be able to take with you if you should retire early. And, look for how you can supplement even that transference.

A word of warning, however: Shop carefully, and comparatively. Make sure, as sure as you can, that you are being protected for out-of-pocket extras and losses, and for unexpected savings invasions. There are too many fast-buck double-talkers promoting health care coverage which may seem inexpensive, but which lacks sufficient protection power. The way to find out which coverage carriers will be best for you is to inquire, shop around, and solicit the experiences of others who have been ill, and have been confined to hospitals. Visiting the sick is charitable if we do not overstay and over-worry them, and we ought to be doing more of it. But if we also observe and listen carefully, we may learn what *we* should be doing in *our own* lives about protection against the cost of being very ill for a long period of time.

Health Insurance Institute statistics show that, today, more than 12 million people sixty-five years of age and over now have some form of *private* health insurance to help take care of costs which Medicare does not cover. If you start thinking, and shopping, for supplementary health insurance coverage, here are some tips from the Institute:

1. Know how long the waiting period is before you will be covered (and *if* you will be covered) or if a preexisting physical condition is excluded in your coverage.
2. Find out if the benefits are limited just to the time you are in the hospital, and how soon they begin their coverage.

3. If benefits are described as a set amount per week or month, calculate what that would amount to per day, and measure that against the *current* daily rate in your local hospital or nursing home.

One way to get ample coverage is through a major medical policy. This type of coverage pays for expenses both in and out of the hospital. It can be purchased before a person becomes sixty-five, and it will be guaranteed renewable for life. There are also a number of companies that offer senior major medical policies for those already sixty-five and over.

Rainy day money ought to be for *living* during those times when sprinkles or showers interrupt our well-being, but the higher cost of a thunderstorm health calamity is another matter. I suggest that it is far more practical to pay an insurance carrier to take care of those catastrophic times than it is for you and I to overstuff our cookie jars with assets we ought to be using to stay involved and really alive.

There are other special coverages: million-dollar policies to protect against devastating disasters, to help shelter us against the real health biggies and their ruinous costs, and some of these also include major medical coverage. There are policies which insure against your having cancer, and which cover you in case you do. Health disability policies are considered by many to be a sensible way to guarantee that you will continue to have income if illness or accident should interrupt your life and regular income.

While we can expect to find reasonably adequate protection in supplemental coverage from among the many types available, there is also the need for using good sense. The absurd idea—and we do see people trying to win in this game—of trying to make money from personal illnesses, is to me a wild and wrong way to place emphasis on being ill. I would much rather bet on staying active and strong from the exercise of living, and to expect to be well for as long as possible. Dr. Bernice Neugarten, the author of *Middle Age and Aging,* said in a Chicago conference in which we both participated, "We must encourage more of our older persons to spend less time and energy in being concerned about their physical selves."

Of course, there are better ways to cope with daily health concerns: The most practical gerontologist I know insists that patients at his institution *do not become senile.* They wouldn't dare. He keeps them active and involved with others. He takes away all canes and crutches that he can. In their stead, he puts the personal and loving touch of a roommate, or of some other patient. He gets his people to stay active—helping each other; going on walks with them for both the activity and the exercise, helping with simple chores, writing or reading letters, perhaps combing hair—staying involved as persons. They soon learn that theirs is not the only, nor even the worst, affliction or condition. He introduces hope . . . and new friends.

It has been my observation, and it grows out of considerable comparison of facilities and styles, that it can be somewhat less terrible to grow old, and less costly, too, if good sense and active sharing is kept alive among the patient population. More appealing and more healthful habits and diets are also helpful, along with the loving expectation that "we here in this special place are going to do all we can to help and uplift, and involve, each other." Upbeat!

Exercises Can Be Simple; Can Help Keep You Fit:

Even older persons, and especially sedentary ones, need the energy-sustaining, life-energizing vigor and strength which comes only from keeping our muscles and our tissues active and toned-up. Not fancy calisthenics necessarily, but blood-pumping vitality-building activity.

Being overweight and losing strength and stamina are the badges of the unfit and are now recognized as invitations to illness and premature old age. If we do not get and stay in shape we will lose out on the rewarding adventures still ahead. *Physical fitness can be achieved at any age!* Check this list to appreciate what you will gain:

• Increased coordination, strength and endurance
• Increased joint flexibility
• Reduction of minor aches, pains, stiffness and soreness
• Correction of remediable postural defects
• Improvement in general appearance
• Increased efficiency with reduced energy expenditure in performing both physical and mental tasks
• Improved ability to relax and to voluntarily reduce tension

- Improved circulation, heart-pumping power, and the reduction of chronic fatigue

- *What Kinds of Simple, and Easy-to-Do Exercises?* *

- Lie on your back, and raise head and shoulders forward.
- Lie on your side and raise opposite leg five times.
- Lie on your back and do an "angel stretch" with feet together and arms close to your sides; then extending your arms and legs sideways up to five times.
- Lie on your back, bend knees and extend them, up to five times.
- Bend forward and down, up to ten times, as well as you can; try to touch your toes.
- Turn your head from side to side, rotating it up to ten times.
- Extend your arms sideways and rotate them, with palms up, then down, up to five times. Then, bring arms to front, extend them sideways from your chest. Repeat up to five times.
- Press your back to the wall; pull abdominal muscles in. Stay relaxed between presses; repeat up to five times.
- Bend your body sideways, with arms extended overhead, up to five times.
- Walk ahead in a straight line for ten feet; then half-knee bend, up to five times, arms extended forward.
- Alternate walking and jogging—walk 50 steps, and jog 10 steps; repeat, up to three minutes.

As in all exercise programs, the advice and consent of your doctor should keep you on safe and sound grounds. If you have a handicap, or are otherwise limited, your doctor may find that some or many of the exercises suggested here—perhaps with modifications—could still be of value to you. Especially in health matters, we cannot look only to others, the medical team and system, but must more and more strive to look to our own resources. We *can* help ourselves with the pressure of health cost inflation as reality keeps crunching and munching on so much of the profit and progress of our hard-working lives, on the substance that we had expected to live on.

*These exercises are approved by the President's Council on Physical Fitness; and they and more are contained in a manual you can order from the Superintendent of Documents, U. S. Government Printing Office, Washington, D.C.

We can, for example, eat less, drink less, and love others more. And we ought to spend less for things we do not really need and which will only clutter up our lives.

For myself, and I hope for you, we can determinedly opt for the sound sense and good habits which will provide vigorous and vital good health for a longer and longer life. Staying well—at least reasonably well—must be our best available alternative; to keep our creaking health machinery running as well as the years and the scars will allow. Living—positively!

Ultimately, in a strictly practical way, we must face up to what most of us are reluctant to acknowledge, and that has to do with the fact and the cost of our dying. Shop around among your neighborhood morticians and you will discover—though it should not be much of a surprise to you—that it appears to be cheaper to hang in there, to stay alive, than to finally shuffle off to your friendly undertaker. *But, even here, we have choices.* There is cremation; this is not a total "freebie," but it does cost less. There are also cooperative funeral facilities which are said to save on cost; and there is that wonderful sharing of leaving either our body, or at least our major organs, for the living use of science, and for that unseen neighbor whose own life may then be extended by our painless contribution.

There is insurance available to cover the cost of our dying. Not just cemetery burials anymore, but mausolea, too. If you happen to be interested in making organ or body grants, find out what is involved well beforehand. Find out what you must *now do* to make such commitment or contractual arrangements: what you will be asked to sign; and what must your survivors know for their guidance at the time of your passing.

And now on to other shockers: For your survivors, there will be less social security income and also less in pension benefits. In most cases, *there will be less* money coming in. Depending on which spouse dies first, and on what insurance coverage you own, there will probably also be less insurance protection to fall back on later, although there should also be less need for it. In many cases, there may be less than enough insurance to cover final illness and burial—especially if the wife (usually less well insured) dies first. And, all too often these days, there is apt to be less than enough cash to handle all those brand new and surprising death and inheritance taxes, which will promptly require payment. These are, indeed, new times, and we had better look ahead and plan ahead to take some of the unnecessary shock out of the end of our lives. Beyond these, and all those other details we should tidy up now, there is always the very practical need for *ready cash*—cash for everyday living, both for him and for her—separate checking accounts from which "living cash" may be extracted, without question or comment, for that or for other emergencies.

Tell your people how absolutely strapped I was—strapped for pocket and grocery cash—when my wife died unexpectedly. They always expect the man to go first; they tell wives to arrange for such separate checking or savings accounts . . . but at our house, my wife went first and it was I who got caught with only ten dollars in my pocket. It was quite a scramble to get enough cash in those first few weeks to do all that I had to do. Tell everybody, wife and husband, and separate individuals, too, to get your own cashable account—for those emergencies which have a way of dumping their problems into our lives.

So spoke Ted Beyers, with the bitter voice of shocking experience.

These reminders, some of them more grim than you may like, are being raised to get your own thinking machinery in gear, and to enable you to tune up for your aging journey. The experience of so many others insists that this does seem to be the better way to go.

As if our expected retirement is not enough trauma for those of us who still resist the promising pleasures of this new living time and this new way of retirement life, some of the rest of us may be getting dumped from our career jobs, unexpectedly, and *ahead of schedule.* This is certainly the kind of surprise party to which no one wants to be invited. Give just a brief thought to how you might cope with such sudden costs (and nightmares) of growing older in that kind of a hurry.

Sidney Williams got canned by his company without warning, about a year ago, after thirty years as developmental chef for a fast foods packager in Philadelphia. Williams was wiped out; he was psychologically destroyed by his company's clumsy handling of his situation. The problem, and there is little point in getting into it, had to do with Sidney's old-line approach, which was in conflict with some of the newer, more academically trained dieticians, young people who were enthusiastic and full of bright new ideas, and who grew impatient with Williams's ways. Management, as it does so logically and so often, bet on the future of youth, and they dropped Sidney from his life's work at the awkward age of fifty-six.

That such a catastrophe is increasingly common these days can be of no comfort to Sid Williams. When he turned up in the hands of a management survival specialist, his only posture and attitude was that his career employer had just killed him, literally.

"I'll be dead in less than two years, and that's for sure. You'll see—two years."

Call it Sidney's justification, or his failure-prone death wish. Call it by any other handle you want to hang on it, this dumping of the near-to-older worker goes on in company after company these days. There are pious corporate rationalizations about why workers are dropped—cash-flow problems, profit crises, pension fund cost trauma. Finally the company may feel forced to take an action, and it happens, all too often, to an older worker who is simply not willing or able to adjust, to keep up or shape up, or to try new ways and new ideas.

No matter what the philosophy, Sidney Williams has just become unemployed, and for the moment, at least, largely unemployable. So the company is killing him in many cruel ways. Or, he is killing himself because he cannot, or will not, accept any part of the blame for his own failure. But, the new breed of modern rehabilitative, outplacement professionals are mighty smart and effective. They help cool a guy down and try, next, to pick him up.

"What else did you do before you headed that fast-food developmental department? What else could you switch to—to start doing now?"

"What else, hell, I gave the company my whole life; it's all I know. Everything I ever worked on, and developed, I gave it all to them. Sure, they paid my salary, but now they robbed me of my reason for living. They stole my chance to do what I do best."

"Yes, but what else have you ever done—in school, in your younger days, in earlier jobs; things you enjoyed and were good at?"

"Way back, when I was just beginning in the creative food business, I had jobs making fancy party specials for big clubs, but nobody can afford costly stuff like that anymore; takes too much time, costs too much. Nobody cares like that anymore. It's all portion-control and fast food today."

"What else, Sidney?"

"When I was a real apprentice beginner, I carved ice sculptures."

"Ice sculptures? That sounds like a pretty special skill."

"Yes, real ice sculpture, and I was good at it too. You know, deer, fish, a bride and groom, or maybe a swan; whatever struck the customer's or the chef's fancy."

"Can you still do ice sculpture, Sidney?"

"Haven't done it in years, but that skill stays if you were good at it. But nobody pays for work like that anymore. The clubs won't try to sell it and the customers don't care for all that stuff anymore."

But, help was on the way. Sidney Williams did get busy: first with sessions with the company relocation "shrink"—the company pays stiff fees for this skill out of corporate conscience budgets; it wanted Sidney Williams off their minds, reestablished in some other place. Meanwhile, the professional counselor dug around—in Sidney's head and among club party contacts—to learn about Sidney's chances to market such special skills: to prepare Quiche Lorraine, Cherries Jubilee, really successful Baked Alaska, and Lord knows what else. A club chef said, "Sure, send me such a guy, and if he can do it proper, I'll get him plenty of work. And also that ice sculpture—sure, we can sell that for special parties; our ladies keep vying to out-entertain each other. Send him to us, soon."

Sidney Williams got so busy carving and turning out fancy foods and creating exotic treats for parties and dinners—and for good fees, too—that he started missing out on a fair number of his scheduled counseling sessions with his so-called "rehabilitator for redundant executives."

Sid did get happy, and confident, once again. No more talk about the company killing him. But, we all know that not every dumped middle- or upper-management guy or gal can find the way back to successful and constructive employment; and not every company will pay the price to see their discards get started on the road back.

The truth is, job security is dead; either we have it in our own heart, head, or perhaps, in our gut, or we don't have it at all. We may as well face this new reality: security is our business. It is our task, and our choice to prepare ourselves for it; we are our own security system. It matters little how much we fear these surprise catastrophes, how much we are certain that our money will run out some day; we will certainly not go hungry or die of starvation.

"We always seem to worry about the wrong things," insists Doctor Hulda Epstein, now a seventy-year-old who lives relaxed in her small Midwestern lake home. Hulda is a retired physician and psychiatrist. She was recounting her experiences of having lived through both World Wars in Berlin, Germany—as a very young girl in the first war, and as a young Jewish professional in Hitler's time. She says that they feared less about getting killed than about starving—during both of the wars. Always fussing about the wrong set of worries. Sure they were concerned about what Hitler was doing to her people and to their country, but they really worried about eating or not eating. She admits that they were often hungry, and mostly poorly fed and not well nourished; but, they always found something—they always ate.

Eventually, she did end up in Dachau and she was moved later to still another concentration camp; and she quickly admits "that it is, it must be, a miracle," for this Jewish professional to have survived, and to be still alive, and even happy. Dr. Epstein strongly admonishes me to tell all of my readers that, in Western cultures, you will not starve. Society does not permit it. When the hungry become identified, and their hunger becomes known, we all rally round, with collections and with a generous sharing. So why, Dr. Epstein wants to know, do we always worry so fiercely about what we will eat—about our material needs and wants?

Philosophy is okay, as long as we can afford it, but it is far more practical to face up now to *what is coming in* and *what will be going out*. We should find out if there will be a serious gap between what we have and what we need, and we should get at this research as early as possible, while we can still take steps to plug up most of these voids. You were shown in a previous chapter, that "income keeps on coming," and it often comes far beyond our fading appetites and our energies to consume it all.

To help guide you in gathering the facts and details about where your money will keep on going, how much it will take to keep your own personal wolf tranquilized, and, in addition, how to make your retirement years a more comfortable and secure sanctuary, we have prepared the "money-needs" chart. It will help you to separate theory, and wishing, from practical reality.

Your Monthly and Annual Money-Needs Exercise Chart

To assess your expenses, now, and after retirement, first read over all of the items. Add any which have been omitted. Cross out those which do not apply to you. Second, check those which are more or less fixed, such as mortgage payments, insurance premiums, or perhaps, rents. Fill these in first, and proceed.

Expenditures	Monthly Average	Annual Average
SHELTER		
Rent	$ _____	$ _____
Mortgage payments	_____	_____
Real estate taxes	_____	_____
Insurance	_____	_____
TOTAL		
HOUSEHOLD MAINTENANCE		
Repairs, house and grounds improvement	$ _____	$ _____
Utilities: water, gas, electricity, etc.	_____	_____
Fuel	_____	_____
Telephone	_____	_____

Expenditures	Monthly Average	Annual Average
Waste disposal	———	———
Services: cleaning persons, cook, gardeners, etc.	———	———
Other	═══	═══
TOTAL		

HOME PURCHASES

Furniture and fixtures .... $	———	$ ———
Floor coverings	———	———
Cleaning and laundry equipment and supplies	———	———
Linens, draperies, shades, etc.	———	———
Kitchen equipment	———	———
Garden equipment, plants, seeds, fertilizers, and patio things	———	———
Other	═══	═══
TOTAL		

AUTOMOBILES AND TRANSPORTATION

Monthly portion of purchase price .. $	———	$ ———
Repairs	———	———
Gasoline, oil, lubricants	———	———
License (drivers and registration) ...	———	———
Insurance	———	———
Other transportation: railroad, bus, subway, plane, taxi, limo	═══	═══
TOTAL		

FOOD

Food at home .... $	———	$ ———
Food away from home	———	———
Liquor and food for entertaining ...	═══	═══
TOTAL		

Expenditures	Monthly Average	Annual Average

CLOTHING

New clothing for all household members .... $ _____ $ _____

Laundry, if not done at home ...... _____ _____

Dry cleaning .... _____ _____

Shoe repair.................... _____ _____

Other .... _____ _____

    TOTAL

PERSONAL

Cosmetics and toiletries .... $ _____ $ _____

Barber shop and beauty parlor ..... _____ _____

Smoking supplies................ _____ _____

Stationery, postage .... _____ _____

Other .... _____ _____

    TOTAL

MEDICAL AND HEALTH

Medicine and drugs.............. $ _____ $ _____

Doctors, dentists, optometrists ..... _____ _____

Hospitals and nursing facilities ..... _____ _____

Eyeglasses, hearing aids, etc....... _____ _____

Medical and health insurance premiums .... _____ _____

Other .... _____ _____

    TOTAL

RECREATION AND OTHER

Books, newspapers, magazines .... $ _____ $ _____

Club memberships, dues, etc. ..... _____ _____

Television and maintenance .... _____ _____

Movies, sports events, concerts, theater, etc .... _____ _____

Expenditures	Monthly Average	Annual Average
Hobby and sports equipment and supplies		
Vacations, holiday celebrations, weekends, other trips		
Adult education		
Pets, pet foods and supplies, license		
Contributions		
Gifts		
Other		
TOTAL		

TAXES, INTEREST ON DEBTS, INSURANCE

	Monthly Average	Annual Average
Federal and state income taxes ..... $		$
Personal property, and property taxes		
Interest, amortization of loans		
Life insurance premiums and annuity payments		
Liability and personal property insurance premiums		
Other		
TOTAL		

SAVINGS AND INVESTMENTS

	Monthly Average	Annual Average
Savings banks, savings associations . $		$
Payments into company pensions, and profit sharing programs		
Private purchases of stocks, bonds, real estate, other investments		
Other		
TOTAL	$	$

	Monthly Average	Annual Average
GRAND TOTAL	$	$

Now, transfer the totals for each category to the "Cost-of-Living" chart which follows.

The foregoing money-needs chart shows what you will need—monthly and annually—to meet your expenses. The following chart brings it all together into a monthly and annual cost-of-living budget.

Cost-of-Living Totals

Expense Item	Needed Monthly	Needed Annually
Shelter	$ _____	$ _____
Household maintenance	_____	_____
Home purchases	_____	_____
Automobiles and transportation	_____	_____
Food	_____	_____
Clothing	_____	_____
Personal	_____	_____
Medical and health	_____	_____
Recreation and other	_____	_____
Taxes, interest due, and insurance	_____	_____
Savings and investments	_____	_____
TOTALS	$ _____	$ _____

These cost-of-living totals, for each category, show you the total you will need—monthly and annually—for your lifestyle. As you project these figures into the years ahead, it will be practical to build in an inflation factor; use an averaged percentage.

The income expectation chart which follows will show what you will, or expect to, be taking in as income from all sources; that still being received from your career activities, and that which will start being received once you have retired. Include any new income sources and amounts, including new mini-career activities.

Estimated Personal and/or Family Income Totals

Income item	Expected Monthly	Expected Annually
Wages, salaries, fees, commissions ..... $ _____		$ _____
Deferred compensation; residual income . _____		_____
Social security benefit income		
Amount husband will receive .... _____		_____
Amount wife will receive .... _____		_____
Company pension payments		
Amount husband will receive .... _____		_____
Amount wife will receive .... _____		_____
Annuities .... _____		_____
Veterans benefit payments .... _____		_____
Company profit-sharing payments ...... _____		_____
Dividends from stock, other investing ... _____		_____
Interest from savings, other sources .... _____		_____
Government, corporate, other bond income .... _____		_____
Interest from mortgages, loans held .... _____		_____
Rents and royalties, other fees .... _____		_____
Profits from sale of real estate, stocks, bonds, other investments .... _____		_____
New income, from new job or hobby activities .... _____		_____
Continuing salary, fees, deferred income from your own business .... _____		_____
Any other income .... _____		_____
.... _____		_____
Any expected new income .... _____		_____
.... _____		_____
TOTALS	$ _____	$ _____

These income amounts show how much income you may be expecting—monthly and annually—to support your cost-of-living. As you project this income for each year ahead, it is practical to build in any cost-of-living indexing increases you can foresee, and also any added income resulting from appreciation of the worth of property you own.

If your cost-of-living chart results do not match up with your income expectations, there are always some actions you can take: (a) you can seek added new income sources, if that is practical; (b) you can begin to cut down on the cost of your living; or, (c) you can start the process of converting some assets into income, if that is necessary and wise.

Each individual and family circumstance is always different; people and their wishes differ. For this reason, it is always prudent to seek counsel: go to your accounting or your banking adviser; check with your attorney or estate planning professional; check with trust people who are familiar with your situation. And, counsel between your selves. What do you want to do? What can you do? What *will* you do?

Certified public accountants are handy fellows—not only can they make calculators hum, keep books, and do audits, they also give sensible business-like advice. One told me to keep monthly and annual income expectations charts and to match with this another monthly cost-of-living expense chart for each year. And then, having set me up with copies of such forms, which anyone can purchase from office supply stores, he suggested that I pay monthly or at least bi-monthly attention to cash-flow and cash-need gaps. The reason for this is that not all income arrives monthly but may be received quarterly or even semi-annually. Likewise, not all bills always arrive month-by-month, but they need to be anticipated and matched up with income due.

I can say for this simple keep-track system that it shows our family if and when income is falling in step with out-go; it gives us either warning or comforting advice. The charts can be homemade or purchased. But they are valuable and most easy to keep, and they'll keep you out of cash-crunch trouble. Fix up your own set, and let them guide your monthly money business.

This is a by-the-month extension of the foregoing money-needs chart materials; or another way to keep income and out-go relationships in clearer focus.

Your Monthly and Annual Income Expectations for the Present Year

Project income expected from each and all sources; List it by months, and total the annual amounts expected for both spouses.

MONTHLY INCOME

Sources	JAN	FEB	MAR	APR	MAY
Social Security SSI: supplemental SS Pension fund payment Profit-Sharing payout Deferred income; Other:	$	$	$	$	$
Annuity payments Disability payments Any other guaranteed income sources:					
Any earned incomes Settlement fees, etc.					
Rental income expected Royalties; Licensing Any other fees, etc.					

Sales of collectibles
Buying or selling
  (Real or other property;
  Property disposed of)					

Inheritance income Alimony payments Dependency income					

Investment income
  Government issues
  Bonds
  Stocks (list them)					

Other interest due Other dividends due					
TOTALED BY MONTHS	$	$	$	$	$

JUNE	JULY	AUG	SEPT	OCT	NOV	DEC	ANNUAL TOTAL
$	$	$	$	$	$	$	$
$	$	$	$	$	$	$	$

ANNUAL TOTALS $

Your Monthly and Annual Cost-of-living Expense Expectation —for this Year

Project your expenses, from this book's lists, and from experience; List by months; and total the annual amounts needed:

MONTHLY EXPENSES

Due to be Paid Out	JAN	FEB	MAR	APR	MAY
Food, regular	$	$	$	$	$
Food, entertaining					
Housing, rents or mortgage payments					
Costs of auto					
Costs for gasoline					
Other transportation					
Health insurance Medicare Supplemental coverage					
Other health care					
Clothing, purchases					
Clothing, maintenance					
Recreational costs					
Vacation trips					
Home, maintenance					
Home, furnishings					
Church and charities					
Personal needs					
Financial expenses or savings set aside Insurance payments Interest payments Loan payments Taxes to be paid, Income Taxes, Real estate taxes, Gift taxes due					
Support payments					
Any other expenses					
Purchases, New auto Second home Boat or other RV					
Contingency, expected or unexpected Being-Nice-to-You, Special trips or other treats					
TOTALED BY MONTHS	$	$	$	$	$

JUNE	JULY	AUG	SEPT	OCT	NOV	DEC	ANNUAL TOTAL
$	$	$	$	$	$	$	$
$	$	$	$	$	$	$	$

ANNUAL TOTALS $

How is your economic vigor now? Are you living on the plus side of life's ledger, or could you still use some help—a higher voltage cash-flow level, perhaps, or a lower level of cash-needs? You may want higher cash flow for comfort, for easing vague worries, or for those extras you have been promising yourself, or lower cash needs for greater safety and peace-of-mind. If there is a gap you wish to or must close; if there is an income increase need or desire, then what are your options for doing anything about it?

There are principally two main choices available: We earn a bit more to fill in the valleys of our wants—constructive, do-able things like earning some extra, mini-career money (will be covered in detail in a later chapter). Or, we can try to find ways to pay out less. One such way is to go hunting for retirement activity and buying bargains. Just today, for example, I signed up (for myself and spouse) at our county courthouse in the senior citizen county-wide discount organization. My wife and I now each have a universal (throughout our county) discount card which is good for from 5 to 50 percent discount on purchases, or services, at well over one hundred area business establishments.

For just one example of how it pays off, a friend bought new eyeglasses recently and the price was about as exotic as the frames—$115. With his new universal discount card, he reduced the cost of his new glasses to $97.75. And anyway you look at it, that is a discount of $17.25 which my friends used to take each other out for a fine dinner.

There is so much more: Last night Mike and Ann Conners took a couple of retired friends to a movie; regular admission was $2.50 each. The four of them were admitted for four dollars total, on senior citizen ID cards.

Last week Mike went to his county courthouse and was enrolled in a free lifetime fishing-license club for seniors, and now fishing will be free for Mike anywhere in his state. Next day, he was out digging for worms. The fish didn't bite much but the day's outing was fun—and cost him nothing.

Last month Mike and Ann stayed at one of those new discount-priced motels along a freeway they travel on vacation. They were pleasantly surprised to have 10 percent taken off of their motel and food bill because that motel group, like so many today, give a senior citizen ID discount card. And this is just the beginning of what the Conners, and plenty of others like them, will be able to tell you about "freebies and cheapies for oldies."

Retired persons have a lot of attractive options going for them that can help hold down the cost of their new life style. They have both the time and the freedom to be flexible. They can take advantage of free days and discount times for special events with admission discounts. These off-peak hours and less busy times are less of a hassle anyway. Going out to eat, or out on the town, "retirement style"— where each individual or couple shares equally in the tab, or pays on a separate check—is a generally agreed-upon practice. This makes sound sense because in retirement it is no longer necessary to put on a "big show" for business reasons.

Not that retired persons will want to, or should, become scroungers, or that most must pinch every penny. That is not a nice way to live all the time, yet, it is sporting activity to keep track of where the best prices, the best times, and the best deals are. You will have time now for shopping around, for being aware of community efforts to do something for senior citizens. And, with compatible friends, these can be extra fun treats, not just free goods or free admission. At the Edison Mall in Fort Myers, Florida, nurses take blood pressure readings for one dollar. There are free glaucoma, hearing, and diabetes check-up clinics at certain times in other localities. It is a good idea to take advantage of these services to get updated reports on life-threatening conditions and on risk potentials.

Dr. Homer Eckbloom went back to school—at age seventy-four. His avocational passion is ceramics. Now he attends a local college and studies with the area's best pottery specialist. Homer pays no tuition because his college is one of more than 500 across the country that welcomes retired students to a widening variety of course disciplines without admission charges.

Going back to school is one of the very best friend-making systems for senior citizens. People with kindred interests study together, share skills, acquire new collaborative friends—at little or no cost. Seniors are advised to check around for subjects offered and class time listings; to get on school mailing lists and stay current on new, special offerings. Seasoned citizens should relax about being "favored" persons. They have long paid their dues as community members and now it is their turn to have special things done for them. Increasingly, smart seniors are getting in on such benefits, which their taxes (heavily weighted with school budget costs) have always provided for others.

In New England, and spreading to other sections of the country, there are exciting new Elderhostel programs which colleges and universities are offering, and which extend the usefulness of idle facilities. With government funding help and for costs as low as $50 for accommodations, short summer sessions (and perhaps other seasons in other areas) these schools are offering special courses appealing to senior audiences. Call them educational vacations—classes designed for adults, inexpensive, and compressed into a week or two. There is no academic credit and no homework, no exams or grades, with no prerequisites, not even high school completion. No one asks and the only requirement is your interest. One retired businessman who attended such a program shared his enthusiasm: "Comparing Elderhostels to previous resort vacations, I'm not sitting around here in a rocking chair just waiting to go in to eat again."

People who reach out and try new things seem to cope best: Marie Halloran is one such widow, and no one ever thinks to feel sorry for her. She is so busy going places, doing interesting things, and always making more new friends. She knows the free days and free times at art galleries and museums; she is up on senior days and special events at ball games and concerts. At local colleges, they think she is faculty because she is there so much for concerts, special art collection showings, and even writing classes. Marie joins others on cross-country trips by bus with more affordable destinations offered than even Marie's considerable energy can absorb, and at modest charges typical for such special tours. On Tuesdays, Marie has her hair done at a nice discount at selected beauty shops or at the local cosmetology college. On Thursdays, she gets her cleaning done at half price at a choice of several dry cleaning establishments.

Eating out is a popular activity in retirement, with busy retirement areas offering "early dining" discounts (and since seniors are most apt to eat earlier, and on schedule, this fits them just fine). Going out to lunch with friends provides a less costly way to eat out, and even to entertain. And since oldsters ought not to eat large amounts of rich restaurant foods too close to bedtime anyway, lunch is often the better idea. Many report finding the late-noon hour, after the crush has settled down, as their favorite leisurely meal time. And, ample lunches cost less than too-ample dinners.

John Morrison suggests that the cost of dressing up in retirement is another cash-flow relaxant. "I never wore a suit but one special day last year. Sure, we dress up pretty sometimes. But we deck out more often in bright, casual sportswear which is fun to pick up on our many shopping junkets, or while we are off on outings. You can be sure we dress up plenty—we went to 200 parties last year."

I am not sure I would be up to 200 parties in any year.

Transportation for retirees, though inadequate in many areas, is also often a cost surprise—especially during off-peak times. Some cities have "dime time" and others issue special ID cards to seniors for discounted fares during hours when passenger loads are light. All this is going on in other countries as well. Switzerland issues off-time half-price fares to older persons for use on its rail systems. In the Netherlands, I met a retired riverboat captain and his wife and long-time riverboat mate, who were off to see the Queen as she opened parliament. They were delighted and proud to tell that they were riding free on what that country calls 65-plus passes. These, naturally, are restricted to certain days and times, but one thing older people are usually rich in is choices of time.

There are so many ways to get smart about enjoying extra activities and events, and to participate at the same time in the happy exercises of stretching retirement incomes. Most daily papers have weekly listings of special events for seniors, places and affairs to go to, alone or in groups, with price details usually clearly spelled out. Most cities now also have an official office called Information and Referral Services. These are fruitful places to pick up all kinds of data that seniors need. Local libraries increasingly list times and places of events—and many of these are special for the later years crowd—on their bulletin boards. Churches, too, offer activities and spread the news of their details. Older persons suggest getting on any promising mailing lists, in order to stay up-to-date.

George Flynn found numerous admission and other price breaks on a recent trip to New York: at the Museum of Modern Art, and later at the Whitney, he noted daily fees were $2 but, as a senior, he was admitted for 75 cents. At one or both of these places, there was also a free day, or a free evening.

As you check in at a Sheraton, a Holiday Inn, or at many of the other hotel/motel chains, ask for their rate, or discount, for senior citizens. Be patient while youthful desk persons sometimes have to check around for what appear to be fluid price and discount schedules. You may be rewarded for your patience with a savings on your stay of from 10 to 25 percent, and occasionally even more.

Seniors get pretty skilled at sniffing out savings situations, and many might justifiably be cautioned about a too strident cheapness, about "always trying to save half of everything for evermore." Living a bit more graciously, and generously, has its own satisfactions, and sharing *is* a beautiful practice, a becoming habit. Being generous to ourselves need not be low on our list, either. The savings rainbow for the older person does have many and varied pots of gold at both ends. But gold cannot be the end in itself. These ideas work best if part of the fun for retirees is found more in the hunting, and less in the catch.

Coping with the cost of growing older can be imaginative and exciting fun; certainly it can be a pleasant pastime, especially when it is part of a sharing experience with friends, or even used for making new friends.

Dr. Richard Schweitzer and his wife, Jane, are from Richmond, Virginia, and their life-long professional and personal friends are Jack and Jeanne Tully. Their average age is sixty. Together, they decided to take an early look at the alternatives they might find interesting for their eventual, and, in their case, welcomed and appealing retirement. They did not wish to wait until it happened to them; they wanted to keep control over more of their own choices. They decided to use their increasing vacation periods for experi-

menting, and for sampling, what their later years could be like. These successful medical friends had been enjoying the good life, professionally and personally, and every winter they would duck off to a high-rise oasis on the Gulf coast or the ocean, or they might take off on a cruise through the islands, where they would laze away the days. Money was not much of an object for them—not yet. But they were not sure how things would be when their money-machine stopped paying off. So, they tossed their money around, and always had a very good time together.

Somewhere around their sixtieth years, they toyed with the idea of doing some test-runs, of trying out retirement living, while still working, and earning. As doctors, they knew a great deal about high living and its cost, physically. They knew they would have to settle on simpler living regimens that would cost less, and decided they ought to look into such possibilities. They switched from plush cruises, with overeating and other indulgences, to the tramp steamer way, for the deck exercising, for the somewhat simpler fare (though not all their tables are that simple). They also switched from martinis to wine with dinner, and found that these very pleasant alternatives fit their palates just about as well as they fit their "rehearsing" pocketbooks. They realized, too, that they were beginning to replace marbled steaks and cholesterol-rich lobster and shell-fish with other fish, fowl, and fruits and vegetables, which in creative culinary hands, come out with every bit as much the gourmet touch. This program for the Schweitzers and the Tulleys was for two years; it was fun in itself, and a happy revelation. They have moved their retirement plans to simpler, less costly, but in no way unattractive, housing along a golf course, and adjacent to fishing lake country. They now seek the active, physical life of biking, hiking, golfing, tennis, and maybe some fishing when these other activities pale.

Okay, you say, it is fine and dandy for fat-cat doctors to traipse off on fancy, costly cruises, living high off any old hog, anytime, anywhere. But for you and your realities, life is, indeed, quite different.

Contrast, then, with these Virginia medical persons, the Mid-America, Mid-South, blue-collar plant worker with most of the same concerns, and some of the same look-ahead yearnings. In both cases, these couples wished to check out of the system, and into social security, at or just past age sixty-two. The first thing the Ludwigs, Phil and Edna, had to do in their preretirement rehearsal experiment was to decide to separate from some of their highest-flying friends, people they might not be able to afford very often anymore–and who, on just a little reflection, they decided they never cared all that much for in any event. The Ludwigs took off from time to time on vacations and long weekends; camping and trailering, visiting state and national parks. They had learned of the availability at age sixty-two and over of a lifetime Golden Age Passport which made the national, and some state, facilities open to them at retirement for no charge or for minimal charges in a few cases.

They also discovered that the larger motel organizations sought their business, and they enjoyed lower rates as "retired persons." There were lower bus fares, and classes for senior citizens without any payment at all. But most of all, they discovered that with their stated intent to "rehearse beforehand," and with their mutual sense of humor, they were enjoying the adventure of discovering how to make their later years a fun-filled and growth exercise. They grew eager to reach age sixty-two and begin full-time their new career of having no specific job or duty. They did learn how to cut money corners, how to enjoy the challenge of making-do, of coping with the costs of their growing-older years.

These are not the only couples I could tell you about. But whether you prefer the style of the Schweitzers and Tulleys, or whether the Ludwigs are more like you in their approach, the comforting truth is that there is, in these methods, some hope and encouragement so that you, too, might work out your own ways of coping with your later life style.

I so often witness sincere and happy people—prudent and affirmative persons—who enjoy trying out ways of coping. On the other hand, all too often I see good people who are endlessly putting it all away for that "rainy day."

I like the sage satire of the newspaper cartoon which teases that "nowadays, the only thing most people put away for a rainy day is their umbrella."

Don't you believe it!

This chapter has had the task of helping unearth where income keeps coming from. It is meant to bring you knowledge about your circumstances and hope for the future. I am not unaware that all of these asset and other income sources and amounts are a highly individual matter. But I have been striving to make you aware of the very real possibility that you may just end up receiving more take-home and more keep-home income, once you are retired, than was ever the case while you were still so zealously career-bent.

The next steps will have to include insights about whose rainy days we are saving it for.

The following checklist should help bring into focus the realities of coping with the cost of growing older. List what you own and what you owe, and what these assets, or liabilities, will either produce for you or cost you.

What You Own

Income These Assets Produce

Assets:	Asset Worth:	Income Monthly:	Income Annually:
Cash on hand .... $ _____		$ _____	$ _____
Checking accounts	_____	_____	_____
Savings accounts	_____	_____	_____
Government bonds, Accrued value	_____	_____	_____
Common stocks, Market value	_____	_____	_____
Preferred stocks, Market value	_____	_____	_____
Other bonds, Market value	_____	_____	_____
Annuities, Face value	_____	_____	_____
Life insurance, Cash value	_____	_____	_____
Real estate, Your home	_____	_____	_____

What You Own   Income These Assets Produce

Assets	Asset Worth:	Income Monthly:	Income Annually:
Other real estate, Appraised value	_____	_____	_____
Automobiles, Market value	_____	_____	_____
Personal property, Household and other	_____	_____	_____
Collections, Antiques and other	_____	_____	_____
Notes, Mortgages held	_____	_____	_____
Pensions, Corpus and income	_____	_____	_____
Retirement trust funds and profit-sharing	_____	_____	_____
Stock options, Any deferred income	_____	_____	_____
Dividends and interest, Other than above	_____	_____	_____
Social security, Corpus and income	_____	_____	_____
Government disability payments expected	_____	_____	_____
Rents, royalties, and any other income	_____	_____	_____

TOTAL ASSETS (what you own)

$ _____

TOTAL INCOME (what you expect to receive)

$ _____ $ _____

What You Owe   **Costs of These Obligations**

Liabilities:	Total You Owe:	Costs Monthly:	Costs Annual:
Current bills . . . . $ ____	$ ____	$ ____
Installment loans . . . . ____	____	____
Contributions, Committed and ongoing . ____	____	____
Mortgage on home . . . . ____	____	____
Mortgage on investment property . . . . ____	____	____
Repayment of loans due on life insurance . . . . ____	____	____
Automobile loans due . . . . . ____	____	____
Furniture and appliance loans due . . . . ____	____	____
Personal loans due . . . . ____	____	____
Hospital, doctor, Balances due . . . . ____	____	____
Support payments and expected obligations . . . . ____	____	____
Other payments due . . . . . . ____	____	____
Balances owing on stocks and bonds . . . . ____	____	____
Payments due on life insurance purchases . . . . . ____	____	____

TOTAL LIABILITIES (what you owe)

$ ____

TOTAL COSTS OF THESE LIABILITIES

$ ____ $ ____

4

Whose Rainy Days Are You Saving It For?

Money is like muck, not good unless it be spread.

FRANCIS BACON,
"Of Seditions and Trouble"

"I hope my dad never hears you talking about 'inheriting his own money.' You see, I'm counting on getting as big a pile of it as I can to take care of *me.*"

This angry and candid challenge startled me; it came from a young university library professional who overheard me discussing the idea of enjoying our own rainy day money with her research supervisor.

Most of the children of retired and aging parents indicate, seeming sincere, that they hope their moms and dads will live it up a bit more; that the old folks *will go* and *do* all of those things for which they never had either the time or the money. Many insist that the finest inheritance they could receive from home would be the memory that their parents were nice to themselves, that they did have a happily fulfilling and pleasant abundance of experiences in their later years.

I am sure there are diverse universes of sons and daughters out there, and that all kinds of views exist on the general theme of inheriting money and property. But, I have discovered that there are monumental guilt problems in many families. I have witnessed that there is great love, and sincere generosity, among many children of older parents; there is also avarice and greed among some of the young families of older persons, and this should surprise no one.

One of the more sensitive morticians of my acquaintance agreed with his pastor recently (and I was startled to hear the strength and universality of their opinion) that, in the case of *too many* burial arrangements, there is present an insistent undercurrent, and sometimes even the noisy expression, of family money and property disagreements. In the midst of their "bereavement" there are whining demands from mousy siblings, or angry outrages from the more aggressive. There are even selfish, guilty, and hateful railings against the departing parent—before the funeral, and long before any reading of the last will and testament.

Perhaps, as the familiar poster suggests, we *should* instead "live long enough and well enough to get to be a problem to our kids."

Becoming dependent is the one most worrisome concern of people who are growing older; they fear the possibility that they might have to fall back on and depend upon their children. But, from extensive observation of today's increasingly affluent society of middle- and upper-income Americans, that old fear of becoming financially dependent upon others is today largely out of step with reality.

"The only real problem with our retirement is that we are accumulating new money." Chuck Hagman surprised me with this fact, and he is far from rare among retirees; his comments are not uncommon for older persons who discover to their delight this very surprising miscalculation.

The truth is—and it is a new and still developing truth—*you may very likely end up with more take-home pay, with more keep-home income, than you had while you were still working—and worrying your fool head off.* Here is how this "problem" comes about: Most of us live out our fearful later lives—and there can be much to be fearful about—sure in the certain knowledge that our days of new income are over once we have retired and are face-to-face with the increasing costs of growing older. Then we discover that it costs us less to live in our years of postemployment than it did while we were still career-bent. As just one example, income taxes, on what used to be "earned income," are all but eliminated for those who *earn* no new income. You can expect to be agreeably surprised that your own projections and income predictions will have been so understated. By instinct and habit we are apt to foresee darkly, and unbelievingly. We will laugh off this new discovery as *a high class problem,* and then we will go right back to protesting that the high cost of living will eat us alive, and that what is left will be rendered worthless by ballooning inflation.

When I told Harold Norton, an old friend from the poor days of long ago, about Chuck Hagman's discovery of their "new money accumulation" experience, Harold sighed with understanding. He told me about the money situation at their house. What he said is typical: social security, that under-rated and too-poorly-regarded basic pension benefit, happens to add up to more than had been expected. "Not that you can live on that alone," Harold quickly added (though I do find many retirees who are managing on it—not wonderfully but not terribly either).

Like Chuck Hagman and Harold Norton, I hope that you, too, will discover that you have been worrying up the wrong tree, that your own retirement income level will also have been underestimated.

Despite all of this, Irene Hagman still fusses at Chuck, "Hadn't we better drop out of the country club, and maybe some other things? We don't need these for business reasons anymore; it costs much too much, and keeps on going up. And besides, we are getting older and use these facilities less. It doesn't make economic sense anymore."

But does it, perhaps, make another kind of sense, this belonging, staying in touch with comfortable old connections, continuing to be involved with familiar acquaintances, keeping current with long-time friends who probably came into our lives from such affiliations? This includes not just clubs, but church groups, card clubs, and former business and trade associations as well.

If there is a consensus among "the disengaged," it is that they too quickly and too finally dropped out of things; they cut off too many of the old reliable avenues to friends, and personal involvements which, good or bad, had always been a large and satisfying part of their formerly active lives. Staying in touch and remaining a part of the lives of old friends and former associates is more significant, and delivers even higher satisfaction *after* we are faced with retirement's threat of isolation. The most successful oldsters tell me they feel better if they stay visible, if they keep on making mental *and* physical contact with people who were vital parts of their years of success and growth. Staying meshed, in functioning step, with such others keeps our own growth—and our human satisfactions—alive and expanding.

Both Hagman and Norton now confess, as still another surprise, that they would have retired earlier than age sixty-five—perhaps at sixty-two—if they had only realized how things would really be, both money and activities. Chuck Hagman would have played more golf, fished, and hunted oftener; he and Irene would have taken off more frequently for their Ozark hideaway.

Norton is a different type, a quiet enigma with a talent in his head and hands. A retired lawyer, he has always painted, mostly prize-winning watercolors.

Now, in his retirement, and at age seventy-three, Norton has still another career going. He is a devoted student in a university art course where he is becoming very good at book-binding. Here, he works with rare leathers, gold leaf and fancy art paper printing stocks. He is a non-paying, non-tuition, senior citizen student.

All the while, the Nortons' portfolio is secure and fruitfully productive, steadily pyramiding their bundle. But, would they ever dig into their ample sock full of assets? Not a chance! Such invasion is completely unthinkable to them. There are no evident heirs; and yet Harold complains bitterly about hop-scotching taxes and galloping inflation, and worries, "What if we should get very sick for a very long time; who would look after us?"

Some time last year, Marcia Norton spotted a special free coupon worth $5 in their suburban newspaper, by which the advertiser was introducing a new car wash and wax service to their community. When Marcia gave it to her husband that evening, she made a tactical mistake. She over-sold that free wash and wax coupon to Harold, and despite the $5 value, and the free coupon, she did not impress her husband very much at all.

Harold slowly, and a touch sadly, pushed that free $5 coupon for that free wash and wax job back toward Marcia. In answer to his wife's question, he said simply that he had been much too poor for much too long, that he had washed and waxed too many cars in his lifetime ever to accept this free one, knowing that it had a regular price tag of $5. And all this, even in the face of their admittedly higher than necessary retirement income, higher than had ever been the case with their regular career income.

There may be understandable reasons for joining today's apprehension generation, but the main point being made here is that we must remain aware that we have choices; that we can still embrace and even cause new awakenings in ourselves. We must acknowledge that most of us continue to have, and that we ought to exercise, a greater conscious and hopeful control over more of our favorable choices. Not just by words of encouragement like these, with an agreeable nodding of heads all around, but with a decision, with a commitment, *to really live*—for as long as we will live.

Whether the sun shines brightly, or there be clouds and rainy days, these *are*, after all, *our* rainy days!

One excellent way to help you decide and check off whose rainy days could possibly out-rank your own, or whose inheritance expectations would even dare rate high enough to get close to, or match, our own, is to chart in graphic form just who rates how high in the heir apparent pecking order in your family. Fill in the names, their logical order of importance, and their rankings on your family's inheritance flow-chart. Do the same with causes and organizations.

Whose Rainy Days? Exercise to Show How to Line Up Heir Priorities

_____
_____
_____
| |
AUNTS   UNCLES   UNCLES   AUNTS
_____ _____   _____ _____
      | |
   COUSINS   COUSINS
_____   _____

                        |
HIS SCHOOL   OUR SCHOOL   HER SCHOOL

      | | |
HIS CHURCH   OUR CHURCH   HER CHURCH

      | | |
HIS FRATERNITY   _____   HER SORORITY
      | | |
HIS SOCIETY   HER SOCIETY
OR LODGE   OR LODGE
_____ | _____
                        |
                        |
        OUR JOINT CAUSES AND CHARITIES

HOSPITALS
_____

SPECIAL HEALTH RESEARCH CAUSES (Cancer, Heart, Kidney,
Arthritis, etc.)
_____

_____

OTHER CHARITIES / OTHER CAUSES
_____
_____
_____
_____
_____

The purpose of such an exercise as this is to help you visualize personal priorities (if there are any, or if there ought to be any to consider), and it can help you decide "whose rainy days" you will want to take into account, and to what degree.

What is suggested here is the setting of person and cause priorities. Number priorities and also indicate the degree of sharing.

It is usually wise to avoid naming amounts, except perhaps in very modest or very large grants. Times change and money circumstances vary markedly so that usually percentages can guide you better in setting shared goals. PERCENTAGES!

In any event, this is simply an exercise to guide your thinking for establishing *your own priorities;* for setting down your own considered opinions about whose rainy days come first, and by how much, or by what percentages. In all such planning, I assume you will be checking everything with your attorneys or other professional advisers. Remember, we are getting involved here in planning part of the process of Inheriting Your Own Money!

As we progress, however ploddingly, groping into the unlighted future of our retirement and aging years, we need to cheerfully keep our wits about us, for who can accurately divine the expanse of those years or know the unexpected cost burdens of new dilemmas? True rainy days are a potential reality. Our automobiles do disintegrate and require replacement; our refrigerators stop refrigerating; washers and dryers and garbage disposal units break down. Even if we are blessed with the heritage of a long life, we too can expect to begin the process of slowly falling apart.

There are few convenient catastrophes—*it really does rain,* too often at the wrong time.

Frank Novak caught me after a TV interview in Indianapolis. He wanted to share the story of what happened to his Uncle Chester and Aunt Millie, and especially, to their late son, Archie. Archie died recently and unexpectedly at age fifty-seven. He had never married, always lived with his parents and had never given them either a care or an anxious moment. Now, they were both eighty-three, and Archie, the light of their lives, was gone. Not untypically, the family had lived hard-working, careful lives, postponing pleasant choices, and accepting self-denial as their way of life in the hope that Archie might have it easier, after they were gone.

But now Archie was gone instead, dead suddenly of an unrecognized cancer. This was obviously a cruel shock to his fine, aged parents. After a time, family and friends impressed on Uncle Chester and Aunt Millie the wisdom of a temporary change; a trip to Florida was advised for both the warmth and the refreshing and pleasant change. They took the bus because it was so much cheaper. Florida was crowded and confusing to them. And very costly. Though warmed by the sun and soothed somewhat by the gentle breezes, all was not well. Uncle Chester's vision worsened—he had been postponing cataract surgery. Because of his increasing discomfort and her mounting concern, they missed out on most of the enjoyment available and decided to come back home far earlier than expected. Everything cost this eighty-three-year-old couple so much they simply could not bring themselves to enjoy anything.

They went back up north, by bus again, to Upper Sandusky, Ohio. On the way, Chester really became quite ill, and Millie was naturally beside herself. But, they did make it back in time to get her husband to a hospital where his health was rebuilt and his vision problems were at least partly corrected. Things are better for them now and they are coping, in their own way.

There is a lesson here for all of us. Even though this nice old couple had always lived out their lives so very carefully, and even though Archie is gone now, there is still no way in which these people can be encouraged to change lifetime habits. The habit of living every day for Archie, of gathering up still more rainy day money, remains. They are simply incapable of doing anything very much different to make their own remaining years any easier or more pleasant. In spite of their own adequate and cautious nest egg, and with no visible heirs to leave it to, there is no way they can comfortably change, even though it has been raining like the very devil lately in their lives.

There are problem days and uncertain times ahead for most of us. There always have been. Today, we have inflation fits and we need to reckon with that reality, positively. Media messages ping away regularly at our already-tightened worry nerves: Will social security funds last, at least until we can get our share of it for when we will need it? Old dogs, it has recently been verified, can be taught new tricks. We can, at any age, continue to grow, to change, and to learn. We may learn a bit more slowly because of our sharpened judgmental skepticism, but we can learn new data. The acquisition of new habits is apparently more difficult—unless we begin the lifetime practice of altering and up-dating our habit-machinery, earlier in our middle and approaching later years.

All around us, there exist thousands of admirable examples of people who go right on living in the affirmative; people who pump most of their energy into doing positive things; people who are taking good care of themselves and being nicer to themselves. But, despite all of our high hopes for better later days, and even in the face of the most well-meaning assurances, we continue to have trouble with our attitudes. We hear the words but we believe they apply to other persons, to other households, to those we too often consider to be so much better off than we are.

Take the case of my good friend, Chris Larstad, and his aging parents. I had never seen Chris so upset before. He was furious with his parents, and sad as hell. He was just back from visiting his beloved father and mother, after some lapse of time.

"My parents are not taking care of themselves. They don't dress well; they don't even eat decently. There's no sign at all of self-esteem or self-concern."

I suggested to Chris that perhaps his folks were ill. He said he didn't think so, but with a touch of bitterness added that they seemed to be working at it: by not eating and not taking care of themselves, surely this would make them ill, in time.

"Nope, I think they're skimping. You see, we were always poor at our house; somebody mentioned it just about every day. And yet, my sisters and I finished college and who do you suppose made that miracle happen if we were so damn poor all those years? I'm really worried about my parents; my sisters and I are going to have a meeting to decide what has to be done."

When I suggested that maybe they really were poor now, Chris laughed a little and then he sputtered again, "My old man is driving around in a 120,000-mile old hack to save his two-year old Plymouth. They sit all day and watch TV—mostly sports, the Twins and the Vikings. But do you suppose Dad would ever take Mom to one of those games just twenty-five miles away? 'It's too far, and what with parking and all, and everything costing so much.' So, they stay home and grow older than their years, and worry us kids like crazy.''

Chris said he had done some digging around to find out if his parents could manage to get along. This is what he found: The Larstad family had moved around, within their town of 5,000, from one cottage to another, and on to still another; they always fixed up house and yard, papering, painting, gardening, and all that. Chris had thought they had sold each home and bought the next, a slightly better one, to move into. Fact is, they never sold any of those earlier homes, just fixed them up and put them up for rent. Four, five, or six houses, all modest but still producing.

Besides that, the senior Larstad had a Railroad Brotherhood pension, not a big one but regular monthly income, nevertheless. After he left the railroad, he worked for some time at a local filling station and picked up his social security credits. Chris's mother had a very modest teacher's retirement income, and after the kids left home she clerked for a time in the local dry goods store, picking up her own social security, however small that must be. So, they do have income. Rental income, and retirement benefit income, plus some asset income.

Chris said his parents were sixty-nine and seventy; he never could remember which was which. They were hardworking and thrifty all their lives, always squirreling away things, always saving money.

''Would you believe I discovered that my sweet old man and my mom have a total income at this time of between $700 and $800 per month?''

I agreed that the Larstads surely ought to be able to get by, and even live quite well in their circumstances, on $700 to $800 per month.

Once more Chris exploded, ''You're damn right they should—but not if they insist on always saving half of everything they get their hands on.''

There is a bittersweet ending to the saga of the Larstad

parents. They did listen to their concerned children with love and a new understanding; they did begin again to "take better care of themselves." They ate better, and dressed up, and went out more than they had been doing. Through their local Sons of Norway, they enrolled in a course to rekindle their native but forgotten Norwegian language—thinking it would be nice to go back to the Old Country, before they died. They even went to some Twins and Viking games. Everything is so much better, Chris happily reports.

Except that the trip to Norway is off. Apparently they waited too long; their legs grew too unsteady, and Mrs. Larstad now has an elevated blood pressure problem; they ought not to risk it. It just go too late in life for all this new living.

Whose rainy days are *you* still saving it all for?

In most well-ordered families, and there still are some, the kids are long gone, on their own, and managing in their way. They worry about the old folks: are they alright, are they well and sufficiently provided for? The children seem to get their greatest jollies out of seeing vigorous and vibrant Mom and Dad living it up a little; they watch with respectful envy while the old folks reach out and touch new life, sampling new experiences. There seems to them to be hope in that; it is the very best and most encouraging example for younger families. There is hope—so that they might strive, and do as well.

The ironic reality about inheriting our own money appears to be the very great difficulty we have of ever, both practically and comfortably, *getting down to our own rainy day money.* This is the result of two principal interferences: new money and new savings have a happy habit of continuing to come in. Our own carefulness and our long-standing saving habits remain just that—ingrained practices which are hard, if not impossible, to break. So, except for major catastrophe, we keep right on growing fatter in purse and property and, for most, there are few really rainy days.

But there are other, less favorable agents at work, as destructively busy as termites. These are the taxing systems which invade our private worlds. They are a resolute lot and their world-wide aim is the redistribution of all wealth. Some bigger holdings probably ought to be sliced and divided and redistributed, to give the truly underprivileged a chance to make a better life. Most of us buy that principle in a general way, just as long as "they" don't try to slice up and divide our particular pile. But they are, and they will!

Gary Turner wanted to know, after one of my lectures, whether he ought to begin leaving some of his net worth to his children, and I reminded him of what many psychiatrists have insisted: that you shouldn't hold out too much hope for the expectation of inheriting money, especially not too early in the lives of our children.

Turner told me that he had always had these same reservations until something sad and unexpected happened in his family. Mrs. Turner had recently died, totally unexpectedly. The family had always lived in Danville, Illinois, but because of a special health situation, their doctor sent them to Indianapolis for special treatment, and for periodic therapy for Helen Turner. They had to go there frequently, so they took a modest apartment where she could live, and where Gary could join her occasionally. This worked out quite well until the moment she died. Gary was there with her.

The mortician came and, upon leaving, asked Turner what their address was. Gary, understandably distraught, gave the undertaker the address of this apartment: 213 Pennsylvania Avenue, Indianapolis. But, the family really lived on Vermillion Street in Danville, and had always lived there.

Now, both states are claiming the Turners as residents and both jurisdictions are pressing tax claims on the Turners' property and on that part of their joint assets which now, upon her death, are becoming taxable. There are costly attorney involvements in both states; there are time-wasting trips back and forth; there has been deposition of witnesses in both communities. In other words, there is a costly and totally surprising mess which will end up taxing, and costing, the Turner family an unfair and wasteful amount of their otherwise secure estate residue.

The question of whether the Turners should begin leaving some of their net worth to their children turned out to be academic, and had to be postponed anyway. If both states do nail them for death taxes, and for all that inheritance assessment trauma, there will probably be an appreciably smaller bundle to distribute.

So go the vagaries of our unseen futures, unless we take excessive care and seek extensive, and regular, professional guidance and see that what *we want* to happen will happen. Let those tax persons wail with their emptier bucket; they will get enough in any event. While I view "their rights and duties" as necessary, I guess, I would rather they didn't sit in the front row, among any other real mourners, smiling expectantly.

Happily, the likelihood of living a long time in our older years is very real indeed. There is a reasonable risk that each of us will grow into the age of infirmities. As the doctor chided me recently, when he poked and prodded about a modest hearing aberration, "If you're lucky, you'll probably get cataracts, too." I asked how that could be any kind of luck and he smiled and replied, "If you live long enough." More and more of us *are* doing just that. But then, there is also the certainty that regardless of our longevity, we all live with something terminal, but as the doc said, "We just don't know it yet."

Whatever our view, and whatever we do about it, there are in these family and personal planning matters, certain housekeeping details and routines which cannot prudently be left to anyone else—not if we want to be sure that *our* wishes will prevail. Before we even know clearly what our wishes may be, we should get our family records organized and straightened out. There are some facts of life we can still do something about, if we know what those facts are. One of the first of these facts has to do with who is in charge at your house. Which spouse, or both spouses together, or which of your children, even if they are long gone from home? Do the kids still exert a real influence on what you do, as individuals or as a couple? Are there friends with strong influence? Are there voices *which merit listening to?* Who are your advisers, and what are the facts and details from which they must make their advisory judgment?

Back, then, to the task of fiscal detail housekeeping; these charts and exercises have been prepared to guide you in updating, and in setting your family and personal records straight.

Complete as fully as possible the following report on the status of the specifics of your situation—not necessarily how much, but where things are. List the location of important papers, records, and personal family details. If you fill in these forms now, you will have completed an important step in getting ready for your retirement and for your later years.

Record the location of important family papers: This is a listing of family advisers, documents, papers, and records of importance for understanding and handling the affairs of:_____

_____
(your name and address)

_____
whose home of record is: _____
(where now located)

_____
The first authoritative person (or persons) to contact in case of emergency includes: _____
(name)

_____
(relationship)

_____
who can also be reached at: _____
(address)

_____
(phone)

Attorney: _____

Accountant:_____

Bank(s): _____

Trustee(s): _____

Personal representative, executor, administrator:_____

_____

_____

Doctor(s): _____

_____

Broker(s): _____

_____

Life insurance underwriter(s): _____

_____

Principal records kept at:_____

_____

Safe deposit box(es): _____
Number, and where located:_____

_____

Home safety vaults: _____
Secret drawers:_____
Office safe(s):_____ _____
Trust department of your bank(s):_____

_____

Records to look for: _____
Insurance policies: _____

_____

_____

_____

Wills (his, hers, yours, theirs): _____

_____

_____

Real estate deeds, titles, mortgages, notes: _____

_____

_____

_____

Apartment lease: _____

_____

Cooperative apartment deeds, leases, agreements: _____

_____

Condominium agreements: _____

_____

Mortgage payment records and status:_____

_____

Note payments records and status: _____

_____

Credit payment contracts and status: _____

_____

Loans to others and status: _____
Loans to family members and status:_____

_____

Loans you owe and status: _____

_____

Automobile titles, registration papers, bill of sale data: _____

_____

Stock certificate data, where kept, when bought, loans: _____

_____

Bonds: _____

_____

Family gift records: _____

_____

U.S. Savings Bonds: _____

_____

Income tax records: _____

_____

Property tax records: _____

_____

Other tax records: _____

Pension records: _____

Profit-sharing records: _____

Burial plot deeds, arrangements, other final rite wishes, instructions:

_____

_____

Bodies, organs to science, arrangements: _____

_____

Birth and baptismal certificates: _____

Marriage licenses, divorce decrees: _____

Citizenship papers: _____

Social security records, cards, numbers, other data: _____

_____

Military discharges, other papers: _____

_____

Veterans Administration records (disability claims, rights, coverages):

_____

_____

Retirement records, other data: _____

_____

Who has copies of this list of vital papers, where recorded: _____

_____

Reminders of other family values, records: _____

_____

Adoption records: _____

Agreements*: _____

Abstracts: _____

Collectors' pedigrees, papers: _____

Heirlooms*: _____

Diplomas: _____

Gems*: _____

Household inventory*:_____

Cancelled checks: _____

Valued letters file:_____

Pension certificates: _____

Treasured photos*: _____

I.O.U.s (family, friends): _____

Committed promises*:_____

Other contracts: _____

Certificates of deposit: _____

Court records:_____

Pet pedigrees:_____

Historical papers:_____

Honors records: _____

Passports: _____

Tax receipts:_____

Historical family records*: _____

Rare coin, stamp, collection data*: _____

Medals, awards*: _____

Jewelry*:_____

Keepsakes*: _____

Divorce data: _____

Other agreements*:_____

*Promises are commitments; they are agreements, especially when in writing —though they can be changed, rescinded. However, the promises concerned with here are human and family things: father to son, mother to daughter, and so on. Write these into your wills, or in separate codicils. Neglecting to do this may cause hurt feelings and unnecessary legal squabbles.

Much has been written about the necessity and the practical wisdom of having valid, up-to-date wills for each spouse, or individual. But it is so important we shall say some of it again.

In the state where I live (Wisconsin), it is estimated that six out of every eight people will die without a valid will. Of the few who do die with a will, 80 percent provide for outright distribution (everything to the surviving spouse), the most costly method of leaving money and property.

If you are still living in the land of illusion, if you still curl up in your cocoon of false security and disbelief in the absolute essentiality of wills, and the making of trust arrangements to guard and conserve your "small estate and modest holdings," you are, doubtless, overlooking two very hard realities. The first is that your estate (and that is not a big home in the country anymore) will not be as modest as you might imagine. In fact, you can make quite sure how large or small it will be. The second is that you probably do not fear or understand accurately the true leeching effect of inflation, nor do you read properly the destructive impact of all those "taxes of dying."

Look at wills and trust instruments in this freshly positive vein: Accept the fact—for it is a fact—that with proper wills and trust arrangements to work for you, you will undoubtedly be able to live pleasantly and quite well for an extra year or two . . . on tax savings alone!

Just this recap of your individual or family records should start the wheels turning. But you can begin to see why we need professional advisers to help us sort out our increasingly complicated personal and/or joint estate affairs.

It may help us to look briefly at two types of wills to get our thinking action-motivated. The first is simply a sample form for a very basic will (do not use this form without legal counsel). By the use of a properly drawn will, one that is legally executed, you can see to it that what you have will get to where you want it—to whom you prefer that it be transferred after your death. (See Will A.)

The second is a sample "last will and testament" of a John Doe who, having died without a valid, legal will (in the state of Minnesota), had the state, in effect, draw one for him as a result of his default. Even in this sad and bitter story, (take note that these things would probably never really happen) we can learn more than enough reasons why we had better get cracking on our own wills and other such arrangements.

WILL A

This is a simple example of a will, and is not intended for actual use.

LAST WILL AND TESTAMENT OF

I, _____ of_____
City of _____ , State of_____
do hereby make, publish and declare this to be my last will and testament and I do hereby revoke all former wills and codicils thereto by me at any time made.

First: I desire that my just debts, including the expenses of my last illness and funeral, be paid as soon as may be practicable after my death.

Second: All of the residue of my estate, whether real, personal, or mixed, wheresoever situated, and whether now owned or hereafter acquired, I give, devise and bequeath unto my beloved wife (husband), _____ , for her (his) own use and benefit forever.

(NOTE: If there are children, they should be specifically mentioned, or they may be set aside.)

Third: I appoint as personal representative (executor) of my will my wife (husband); I request that she (he) be permitted to serve without sureties on her (his) bond and that, without application to or order of courts, she (he) have full power and authority to sell, transfer, grant, convey, exchange, lease, mortgage, pledge, or order of courts, she (he) have full power and authority to personal property of my estate.

In Witness Whereof, I have hereunto subscribed my name this _____ day of _____ , 19__ .

The foregoing instrument consisting of _____ sheets was signed, published, and declared by the said _____ as and for his/her last will and testament in the presence of us, who, at his/her request in his/her presence and in the presence of each other hereunto subscribed our names as witnesses.

_____ residing at_____
(witness)
_____

_____ residing at_____
(witness)
_____

WILL B

This could happen if you were to die without a valid will.

LAST WILL AND TESTAMENT

of

JOHN DOE

I, John Doe, of Anytown, Minnesota, hereby do make, publish, and declare this to be my Last Will and Testament.

FIRST ARTICLE

I give my wife only one-third (⅓) of my property and I give my children the remaining two-thirds (⅔).

I. I appoint my wife as guardian of my children, but as a safeguard I require that she report to the Probate Court each year and render an accounting of how, why, and where she spent the money necessary for the proper care of my children. (Applies only to minors.)

II. As a further safeguard, I direct my wife to produce to the Probate Court a Performance Bond to guarantee that she exercises proper judgment in the handling, investing, and spending of the children's money.

III. As a final safeguard, my children shall have the right to demand and receive a complete accounting from their mother of all of her financial actions with their money as soon as they reach legal age.

IV. When my children reach age eighteen (18), they shall have full rights to withdraw and spend their shares of my estate. No one shall have any right to question my children's actions on how they decide to spend their respective shares.

SECOND ARTICLE

Should my wife remarry, the second husband shall be entitled to one-third (⅓) of everything my wife possesses.

I. Should my children need some of this share for their support, the second husband shall not be bound to spend any part of his share on my children's behalf.

II. The second husband shall have sole rights to decide who is to get his share, even to the exclusion of my children.

THIRD ARTICLE

Should my wife predecease me or die while any of my children are minors, I do not wish to exercise my right to nominate the guardian of my children. (Let the court do it.)

I. Rather than nominating a guardian of my preference, I direct my relatives and friends to get together and select a guardian by mutual agreement.

II. In the event that they fail to agree on a guardian, I direct the Probate Court to make the selection. If the court wishes, it may appoint a stranger acceptable to it.

FOURTH ARTICLE

Under existing tax law, there are certain legitimate avenues open to me to lower death taxes. Since I prefer to have my money used for governmental purposes rather than for the benefit of my wife and children, I direct that no effort be made to lower taxes.

IN WITNESS WHEREOF, I have set my hand and seal to this, my Last Will and Testament, consisting of two (2) typewritten pages, all this _____ day of _____, 19___ .

_____(SEAL)

JOHN DOE

© 1976 Estate Research Co. 95003

NOTE: Since the Tax Reform Act of 1976, and since "Fair Market Value" and not *cost* will doubtless be the new taxing basis with which you will have to reckon, you need to seek really competent professional help to get wills made where there are none, and to get all wills updated that were made prior to December 31, 1976.

Granting Power of Attorney

Power of attorney is a written document or instrument by which you, as the principal, appoint an attorney-in-fact to act as your agent, and by which you confer upon him or her the authority to act in your behalf.

Power of attorney may either be general, giving you the power to do almost anything on the principal's behalf, or it may be restricted or special, giving you the power to do only one or more specific things, and/or for a limited period of time, in behalf of the principal.

If you should become incapacitated, have a heart attack, be in a serious accident, or otherwise be unable to manage your own affairs, someone should be authorized to sign checks to pay bills, borrow money if necessary, or file insurance claims, or, someone may need to cover your affairs if you are to be away for an extended period of time. Later on in life, there is the possibility of becoming weak, disabled, or senile, and someone should have the authority to act for you.

Obviously, this is a very great and over-riding power and ought not be granted to less than the most responsible, and close, person you can decide upon. One woman said she is much more comforted by this power of attorney than she is by her will.

KNOW ALL MEN BY THESE PRESENTS: That I, John Doe, of Any City, of Any State, have made, constituted and appointed and by these presents do make, constitute, and appoint Martha Doe, of Any City, of Any State, my true and lawful attorney, but in the event of her death, disability, or absence from Any State, then I make, constitute, and appoint the Any City Bank of Any City, of Any State for me and in my name, place, and stead with full power and authority to allot, assign, borrow, care for, collect, contract with respect to, convert, convey, deal with, dispose of, enter into, exchange, hold, improve, insure, invest, pledge, take possession of, protect, receive, release, repair, sell, sue for, and in general, do do any and every act and thing and to enter into and carry out any and every agreement with respect to my property whether real, personal, or mixed or any part thereof which I may now or hereafter own, to draw, make, assign any and all checks, contracts, or agreements, to institute or defend suits concerning my property or rights, and generally do and perform for me and in my name, all that I might do if present, and I hereby adopt and ratify all of the acts of my said attorney done in pursuance of the power hereby granted as fully as if I were present acting in my own proper person, provided, however, that my said attorney is not to bind me as surety, guarantor, or endorser for accommodation nor to give away any of my estate whatsoever. All acts done by my attorney pursuant to this power during any period of my disability or incompetence or any uncertainty as to whether I am dead or alive shall have the same effect and inure to the benefit and bind me, my heirs, and devisees and personal representatives as if I were alive, competent, and not disabled. This power of attorney shall not be affected by the disability of the undersigned as principal.

WITNESS my signature this _____ day of _____, 19__.

STATE OF _____

COUNTY OF _____

The foregoing instrument was acknowledged before me this _____ day of _____, 19__, by John Doe.

My Commission will expire _____.

_____
Notary Public, Any City, Any State

Power of Attorney—The Basic Form

Naturally, this is but a sample of what a document for power of attorney looks like, and what it can do for you. Have yours drawn by your own legal counsel. Since state laws vary widely, no form such as this will fit just any circumstance, and you are cautioned to seek professional help. There is so much more to the problem or, rather, to the opportunity that you have to conserve your assets and your estate than just the making and filing of a valid, legal will. Even if one or both of you recoil from the very subject, or if you find it a bore and a chore, you will do well to heed the experiences of thousands who lose millions. These are the thousands whose money and property end up in the wrong hands, or, worse yet, in the hands of the variety of tax collectors. Heed, therefore, this estate-planning data. Estate-planning pays off in money and property saved, protected, and properly transferred (with substantial taxes saved), and with *your* wishes followed and adhered to. But first, you must decide what it is that you (each or both of you) will want to have happen. *There is no playing this tune by ear!* You need the best professional counsel you can find, after consulting advisers, friends, and acquaintances. The following are professionally provided guidelines to help you be a smarter planner, and a better shopper for these services:

Estate Planning Guidelines

I. Introduction
   A. Scope of the Problem
      1. Creation (concentrate more on this, and earlier)
      2. Preservation (likewise worth careful concentration)
      3. Disposition (avoid too much disposition emphasis)
   B. Motivation for property transfers (be sure you have objectives—and management)
      1. Gift (honest, sincere wishes)
      2. Bribe (manipulation of recipients)
      3. Self-interest (enlightened self-interest is your very best, most objective motivation)

         a. Creditors (proof; judgments, potential liability)
         b. Wives
         c. Management (preservation, changes, up-to-date)
         d. Protection of family—wife and children (the major factor)

      4. Taxes (they intrude on preservation)

         a. Transfer (gift and estate taxes)
         b. Income taxes

II. Present Estate
   A. Group life insurance
   B. Ordinary life insurance (check your state, some states absolve first $10,000, for example)

      1. Tax savings
      2. Personal considerations
      3. Form of transfer

         a. Outright
         b. Trust (who pays premiums, right to withdraw)

    (1) Costs
    (2) Records (and reporting)
C. Joint property
  1. House (no gift unless elected)
  2. Bank accounts (no gift until appropriated)
  3. Securities (immediate gift, but also includable in estate, best to have in "your" own name)

D. Simple will (from one to thirty-five pages)
  1. Outright to spouse with contingent trusts for children
  2. Administrative powers
  3. Appointment of personal representative: trustee, executor, guardian

III. Planning for Life
  A. Business

    1. Professional incorporation, qualified plan

      a. Income tax deferral
      b. Non-discriminatory
      c. Exempt from estate pensions (leave other than to estate)

    2. Sickness and disability benefits
    3. Deferred compensation (study effect on minimum tax)
    4. Stock options—qualified, non-qualified, restricted

  B. Investments

    1. Tax sheltered real estate; depreciable property
    2. Tax exempt municipal bonds

  C. Gifts

    1. Personal considerations

      a. Control of property
      b. Unexpected order of death
      c. Divorce

2. Tax considerations

   a. Comparative gift and estate tax rates, separately applied

   b. Annual exclusions ($3,000 at present)

   c. Cumulative exemption ($30,000 at present)

   d. Charitable deduction

   e. Marital deduction

   f. Future appreciation (transfer tax savings)

   g. Substituted basis

3. Types of gifts (controlled amounts)

   a. Loans and periodic forgiveness (avoid gift taxes)

   b. Short-term trust—10 years (shift income for later need)

   c. Minority trust

   d. Mandatory income trust, present interest

   e. Long-term trust, shift income and reduce transfer taxes sprinkling (generation-skipping)

   f. Charitable gifts

      (1) Appreciated property

      (2) Pooled income fund

      (3) Annuity trusts and unitrusts

4. Complexities:

   a. Public vs. private charities

   b. Capital gains

   c. Ordinary income property

   d. Bargain sales

   e. Realization of capital losses

   f. Choice of assets

      (1) Depreciated assets: sell, realize loss

      (2) Appreciated assets: loss of stepped-up basis on death

D. Corporate structure—future appreciation, preferred and common stock

IV. Planning for Death

    A. Business buy-out

        1. Methods

           a. Entity

(1)   Source of funds
                (2) Lower basis
                (3) Redemption

           b. Cross purchase

        2. Funding—insurance

    B. Will

        1. Marital deduction
        2. Residuary trust

    C. Estate tax bonds

V. Conclusions

    A. Make plan fit personal objectives
    B. Emphasize creation, and preservation
    C. Consult your attorney

This estate planning guideline information may tell you more than you wish to know on the subject. The best advice for you is to find the best advice possible, for your situation. So much for "rainy day" preparatory record-keeping, however necessary or practical it may be. There are other criteria, other standards for success or failure in one's later years. But you, being of sound mind, and suitably forewarned, know how to pick your own way to go. Not like Elsie Kasten.

Elsie Kasten died a year or two ago, at age eighty-four. She left behind an unresolved neighborhood notions and dry-goods emporium. She also left behind a mess; more of a mess than just those bins of buttons, spools of thread, and tired elastic. The inventory was surely in a mess. Due in part to Elsie's weary age, and to the simple fact that she was a bigger conserver than she was a merchandiser, she had more tired merchandise than traffic. And since

*both the store and its wares were paid for, her store was liquid
even if Elsie Kasten was not.*

*A sister was summoned by merchant neighbors, all the way from
Terre Haute, to take charge after the store had been closed for a
couple of weeks, ever since Elsie died. The sister had to leave
behind in Indiana her own sick husband, and her own unsettled
family financial situation. Martha, Elsie's sister, was absolutely
inexperienced in business, including merchandising. Her only
possible goal in this unexpected situation had to be to empty all
those shelves and bins, sell the building, and go back home
to Indiana, back to her own world of unfinished business. There
were also younger relatives, nieces and nephews, who might have
been expected to lend a hand, to help Martha settle Elsie's affairs. Expectant though they openly were, they were also un-
cooperative, leaving Martha in charge—and in trouble. Even patient Martha began to murmur about Elsie: Hadn't she been
successful all these years? Hadn't she built a successful business,
managing everything well, all by herself? But how come smart
Elsie had never made a will, had never lined up her affairs so that
knowledgeable professionals could have taken charge?*

How come, indeed? And, how come all those other 70 to 80 percent of adults, who have no valid last will and testament, go on playing Russian roulette with all the fruits of their hardworking lifetimes?
Living and working without a will can be oversight enough, but where
there is progress and prosperity, even if it is just in the making, there
should be some kind of fiscal planning.

*One story I delight in has to do with Dr. Antonio Scali. This
wonderfully delightful philosopher has made enormous medical
contributions, almost personally stamping out tuberculosis in his
region. He is still practicing and will probably do so for a very
long time. One can only hope so—for the good of his lucky patients
and charges. Speaking of charges, Dr. Scali always pays cash; he
is about as paid up as one has a right to be. He was brought up to
be thrifty, and happy, and prepared. His loving Italian family
sang songs—passionate, sad, and happy songs—and Antonio*

sings as well. But he is making his money from medicine. (Quite a lot of money, thank you.)

But what does one do with money—and especially money for later life, for those rainy days—when one has come from such a financially inexperienced background? Dr. Scali and his spouse called on their professional advisers. One day he was musing with one of them about whether "putting aside $9,000 each year was enough to be saving." He wondered if his friendly adviser had any idea about what other professionals like himself were saving, for their retirement.

The adviser, a top-notch success in the estate planning area of the insurance business, was more than amazed. He knew from his own case, and from client experience, how tough it is to regularly lay by, or save any substantial amount annually. The insurance professional, and you may fairly say that he did so cunningly, had a suggestion: He thought the Scalis were a bit too anxious, too conservative. Instead of saving $9,000 every year, he suggested instead that they could invest just three thousand of the nine they had in mind; and with it they could buy both life insurance protection, and an annuity combination which, in the end, would pay them back $100,000. For $3,000 annually they bought insurance protection and would own an annuity worth $100,000. For the $6,000 they would not need to put away each year, by this method, the underwriter suggested they take off for Italy, for song singing and heritage hunting, and for living today. Call it a self-serving suggestion if you like, but in this case it was appreciated counsel. It was an appealing alternative they could richly understand, and, besides, it helped them feel less prodigal—it was advice!

So they took the big bird, went to Rome, and stuffed themselves with pastas and heaven knows what else, all washed down with charming Italian wines. They looked at churches and shrines and catacombs. They had a great time, enjoying being Italian—in Italy. And they were not unaware that they could do this and more every year, and still not end up in want come hell, high water, or any really rainy day.

When the Scalis came back, they ran into their estate adviser. They regaled him with all of the news of their Italian, and their

Greek Isle, and their Riviera frolicking. Mrs. Scali stuck her fore-finger right to the nose of Mr. Insurance Man, and, with a wink and a broad smile, said that it was all his fault that they went running off like that, having all that great fun and experience, because "he had told them to."

Dr. Antonio Scali can rationalize it all much better, by quoting what he claims to be an old Italian proverb—but which one suspects he may have picked up from Charlie Brown or from Snoopy: "Making money is like bees making honey; they let you make it, but they don't let you keep it." Not even for a Rainy Day?

5

Never Invade Principal That's Some Principle!

You must leave your many millions
And the gay and festive crowd;
Though you roll in royal billions
There's no pocket in a shroud.

JOHN ALEXANDER JOYCE

We were sitting around the kitchen table arguing, just the four of us: Shirley Deedrik, her quiet husband, Vic, and my spouse and I. Shirley was arguing mightily. She was attacking my suggestion that saved principal need not be forever sacred, despite grandfather's warnings. Principal can, and should be, judiciously programmed into our retirement and later years to help finance and enrich these golden times, if they are to be golden for us.

I interrupted Shirley's strong narrative with the story of Sam Johnson and his wife, Ruth, to make my point.

One day Sam had been in his upstairs bedroom "office" for two or three hours and when he came down for a cup of coffee, Ruth asked what in the world he had been doing up there for all that time. Sam told her simply that he had been making out a net worth statement.

"Go on," she chided, "you do that every day now that you're retired."

"I do not—haven't made up a net worth report in the last year or more, not since we had our wills updated."

"Well, Sam, what does your money add up to; how much is your net worth worth today?" She asked it in a taunting way since Ruth was, in financial matters, no optimist.

"About $150,000 is where our net worth is at, besides the house and our cars and other stuff," Sam responded, and not without some smug pleasure.

"$150,000?" Ruth was unbelieving, but then she faced Sam squarely and challenged him, "Does that mean, Sam, that we could spend $15,000 per year for the next ten years, by which time we'll probably be dead anyway?"

"Yes, Ruth, my skeptic, it does mean that—in a way. It means, to put it another way, that we could spend $10,000 for fifteen years, or $5,000 for thirty years; but there is no need to spend that much, unless we really want to.

"You see, Ruth, as I've tried telling you so many times, that $150,000, or whatever it happens to be, keeps right on earning and increasing. At 7½ percent interest in insured savings certificates, for example, that $150,000 earns $11,250 per year. That's $937.50 per month. We can take all of that extra income, on top of what we already have coming in from our pension and social security, and we can spend and enjoy it all. That $150,000 will still last forever, because, you see, we would only be taking out the interest our money keeps on earning."

That is pretty much the story of Ruth and Sam Johnson and their particular bundle; and about our over-trained reluctance never to touch our principal. This is not an uncommon point of view in most middle- and upper-income households. Shirley and Vic Deedrik heard all of this from me, in great detail, but I am satisfied that Shirley, at least, still holds her grandfather's dictum sacred.

It must be acknowledged that we hold back, both sensibly and conservatively, because we have witnessed all too often the dark days and hardships which have happened where improvidence has reigned. We worry, understandably, about all those things which might happen, even though we are really quite thoroughly cushioned and protected against running out of money. This is especially true for this generation and the years we have left for living constructively.

I must admit that, even as a researcher and an affirmative advocate, I have some apprehensions: I am concerned that good people may misunderstand and foolishly embark on too much risk; and I am also troubled that others will remain too unbelieving. There is a middle ground; one *can* responsibly live it up.

Because of these expressed uncertainties, and especially because I might not be making it all graphic enough, I took the problem to Gill Feller, one of the most conservative, and yet, most progressive trust and investment counselors I could find. I gave him the problem of how prudent individuals and families could "draw down" on both the interest and some principal—from a savings and investment amount of, for example, $150,000—without running into trouble, or running out too soon. We reviewed together that people have choices: They can take only the interest (as in the example of the Johnsons) and never run out of principal; They can relate all this to life expectancy, and using Gerald Loeb's "security method" of doubling the figure of our life expectancy, can draw down, for example, $1/30$ each year (if their life expectancy is fifteen years) without ever risking running short; Or, as Gill Feller demonstrates in the following chart, they can use a combination of the two.

Insured savings certificates, in order to earn their maximum, are required to remain for a total of six years. On a daily compounding schedule, you can earn as much as 7.90 percent (at the 7½ percent rate). You can take that earned interest out once a year, but principal must stay for six years. Now, if you would wish to draw on a combination of that interest and some principal, you would have to buy a combination of 1-year, 2-year, 3-year, 4-year, 5-year, and 6-year certificates, with part of the $150,000 accepting a lower, but still attractive, yield on certificates maturing in less than six years. Such a program could be used to generate over $17,000 per year for fifteen years using a $150,000 initial investment. Follow the charted data and the explanation showing how simply it works.

With the $150,000, you would buy, at the beginning of the year, savings certificates valued at the following amounts; earning at rates listed, and varied among 1-year, 2-year, 3-year, 4-year, 5-year, and 6-year maturities; and producing income as listed.

Table 2

Buy for Year	Value	Rate	Income
1	$ 5,500	6.27%	$ 345
2	5,845	6.27	366
3	6,211	6.81	423
4	6,634	7.63	506
5	7,140	7.63	545
6	118,670	7.90	9,375
	$150,000		$11,560

This is a possible program of rate earnings and income earnings on the varied maturities and on the larger corpus together during the first six years. Also, from the first year on, you can then draw that annual income, plus an increasing amount of principal, to total $17,060 per year from the combination of the interest and the principal.

Table 3

Receive for Year	Principal Used	Income	Total Drawn
1	$ 5,500	$11,560	$ 17,060
2	5,845	11,215	17,060
3	6,211	10,849	17,060
4	6,634	10,426	17,060
5	7,140	9,920	17,060
6	7,685	9,375	17,060
	$39,015	$63,345	$102,360

Note that the principal remaining at the end of the sixth year is still $110,985. And note also that each year's total drawn has remained at the $17,060 amount, which is a combination of a modestly decreasing income level and a modestly increasing principal withdrawal. Now, at the seventh year, a similar purchase of variable year certificates is again necessary as indicated in Table 4.

Table 4

Buy for Year	Value	Rate	Income
7	$ 8,900	6.27%	$ 558
8	9,458	6.27	593
9	10,051	6.81	684
10	10,735	7.63	819
11	11,554	7.63	881
12	60,287	7.90	4,763
	$110,985		$8,298

Continuing this exercise, let us examine again the principal used, and the income earned, to determine what would be drawn from the certificate amount in combined interest and principal. The total annual payout has now increased slightly, to $17,198.

Table 5

Receive for Year	Principal Used	Income	Total Drawn
7	$ 8,900	$ 8,298	$ 17,198
8	9,458	7,740	17,198
9	10,051	7,147	17,198
10	10,735	6,463	17,198
11	11,554	5,644	17,198
12	12,435	4,763	17,198
	$63,133	$40,055	$103,188

Principal remaining at the end of the twelfth year is now $47,852 and this will last through the fifteenth year, and allow annual distributions to increase to about $18,000 during the final three years.

Table 6

Buy for Year	Value	Rate	Income
13	$15,000	6.27%	$ 940
14	15,940	6.27	999
15	16,912	6.81	1,152
	$47,852		$3,091

Table 7

Receive for Year	Principal Used	Income	Total Drawn
13	$15,000	$3,091	$18,091
14	15,940	2,151	18,091
15	16,912	1,152	18,064
	$47,852	$6,394	$54,246

After 15 years you now have exhausted your $150,000 fund, but you did not run out of income or assets. You got your money back and you also received $109,794 in earned income for a total of $259,794. This is one way to go, to invade principal judiciously. It needs to be acknowledged that if your life expectancy should be longer than fifteen years, you would need to draw down less than the approximately $17,000 each year to make the money stretch for some years longer. All these are individual situations. For example, not everyone deals in just $150,000 of investable corpus. There are some people with more, often much more. But there are also a great number of us who may despair at an exercise like this when we have to look pensively at our own $100,000, or even $50,000 of investable assets.

We must also remember that we are talking here of investable capital. We do not include our household, our real estate properties, our insurance—just money available for earning income. And finally, this income demonstration does not include any part of your social security, pension benefits or profit-sharing income sources or amounts.

Consider any such exercise as just that—it shows that we do have choices of how we want to employ and enjoy our net-worth assets. And, even if your savings place does not offer this kind of service, they do have the technology—and most have the sales ambition—so that they can and should make such service available to you. It helps, when we are older, to continue to believe in the positive.

We have a conservative banker in our community by the name of Charley King, but we call him "Cash-Flow" King. Hard-line, play-safe King surprised me recently when he critically took off after some of his fat cat friends and customers.

"It's my own kind of people who upset me the most; always hating all government for all those taxes, and regulations. The only creative thoughts they have anymore is how they can still multiply their already overstuffed assets. They live fearfully, and generally lead largely uncharitable lives. They think I have lost my mind when I chide them for living like Shylock, for refusing to let go of any of their almighty bundle, even in their twilight years.

"Cash-Flow" told me with some chagrin about two of his bank customers: One, a retired, unmarried teacher with no discernible heirs, came to him for investment advice. During the meeting she admitted that she had been building her modest salary for the past forty years, so that now she had something like $400,000 of savings growth and she wanted to know from Charley what she ought to do. Another customer, a postal worker, had pyramided old houses he had fixed up, and other real estate properties he had been trading in, into something approaching a half million dollars, and he came to Charley King for advice.

To his credit, "Cash Flow" admitted to me that he was way over his head with successes like these. He said that if he had been advising either one of these "small town surprises," they might not have done nearly as well. With his conservative advice, they might have been lucky to have earned even 6 percent interest on average. Charley admitted he was scared to make even one suggestion, for fear they would lose their own golden touch. His customers, Charley says, never cease to surprise him with their own "homemade" success stories. He is finally able to ridicule some of his conservative tendencies, and to mock those of his clientele, who just can't squeeze loose any of their hoard—especially their principal.

"Cash-Flow" King told me a banker story—and it may be apocryphal—about a banking acquaintance of his, way up in the woodsy quiet of Maine. This local banker had a younger visitor from out of town, and after their conference, they went out to

lunch in the local hotel dining room. As they walked down the street, they met other citizens and received what appeared to be friendly greetings from all. But the local Maine banker seemed to be avoiding the greetings, steering his younger friend across the street, to avoid direct contact, in what was surely an obvious ducking of proferred cordiality. The younger man asked him why.

"You guys from the city will never understand why I must keep my distance, why I must protect my own banking principles. What you don't know about some of these people is that 'they invaded principal.' "

Jerry Huber is one of the trust officers in a huge Minneapolis bank, and he was explaining to me the day-to-day problems faced by just two of his widow clients, ladies who had been left alone to manage, and to live on what was left of their successful husbands' money.

Their most frequent question was, "What will I live on if inflation and rising costs continue?" These good women have an excessive sense of responsibility to their husbands' lifetimes of saving carefulness. They are afraid of not doing everything right, and Jerry Huber must comfort and guide them—sometimes with sternness. They protest his suggestions for staying more in touch with old friends. "But, Mr. Huber, we don't like to go out much anymore, especially in the evening. You know, something might happen to us, what with everything that's going on." And Jerry has to encourage them to take taxis and to go with another friend, but to stay involved, to keep active with old friends, and to avoid becoming recluses—for all reasons, including health and mental well-being.

One of the ladies told Jerry about what she had been doing— taking down the drapes to get them cleaned. He asked how she did that (she being about seventy-three). "Oh, I just pulled up a dining room chair, unhooked the drapes, and folded them down. Nothing really to it." And she fully expected to hang them back up when they had come back from the cleaners—lifting, straining, standing again on that dining room chair. Well, Jerry Huber gave this lady quite a firm lecture about always living so poorly and so far in the past. He reminded her that at her age, and with her several hundred thousand dollar asset remainder, plus the income it

*kept producing, that she ought to start having someone else do
this reaching and take the risks. Because, as he reminded her—
and all of us older citizens ought to be reminding ourselves—a
fractured hip is the one thing we do not need at our age.*

And yet, we are so much more skilled at saving $15 than we are
at living pleasantly, prudently, and securely, or paying the $15 to
save, maybe, the $15,000 which might be the accidental alternative.
We grow dollar-wise and fortune-foolish. But, who ever said that
older is necessarily smarter? Robert Edwards gave some sound advice
in a special feature in the *Christian Science Monitor,* "Inflation and
Retirement; Spend Some Principal."

Any plan for spending part of your principal stands on three legs:
your age, the amount of money in your savings pool, and how
much your savings earn regularly. *For example, suppose your
savings pool (stocks, bonds, certificates of deposit (CDs), and
other investments) amounts to $60,000. If your savings earn an
average of 6 percent, your income is $3,600 annually, or $300
per month. By withdrawing $3,600 per year or less, your savings
pool will last indefinitely. However, suppose you decide you need
$450 per month, or $5,400 per year; that amounts to a 9 percent
withdrawal each year. Therefore, each year you would be taking
out $1,800 more than is earned by spending part of your savings.
How long will your savings last? According to the following table,
your savings will last 18 years.*

Percent of original principal withdrawn per year:	Average return on principal: (principal will last this many years)						
	3%	4%	5%	6%	7%	8%	9%
4	46	*					
5	30	41	*				
6	23	28	36	*			
7	18	21	25	33	*		
8	15	17	20	23	30	*	
9	13	14	16	18	22	28	*
10	12	13	14	15	17	20	26	*

*Indefinitely: Income equals withdrawal rate.

Suppose, however, that your savings earn an average of 8 percent, instead of 6; you could then draw $450 per month, or $5,400 per year, for twenty-eight years instead of eighteen years, because more spendable dollars are interest and fewer come from principal.

The third variable is your life expectancy. Over-spending could leave you with no savings; but, hoarding by spending less puts a limiting strain on your life style. One rule of thumb in planning a systematic withdrawal of principal is to double your life expectancy. If you are now sixty-eight, mortality tables indicate that you can expect to live another 11.7 years if you are a man, or 15.3 years if you are a woman. To allow a safety margin, you can double these numbers—to 24 years for a man, or 31 years if you are a woman. Plan your withdrawal amounts according to those amounts, and you will not likely run out of money. (Bear in mind, as well, that we are speaking here of systematically, and judiciously, using up your savings pool—interest and some carefully factored principal. This will be in addition to your social security and your pension benefit payments, plus any other income you may have.)

All three pieces to which Robert Edwards referred are now in place, and you can better judge whether you want to spend more during your younger, more active years, and slow down your spending later. Or, you may decide to follow a straight line by withdrawing the same amount every year. Planning to spend part of your principal regularly requires some attention to management, some cautious action by you, but the payoff can be a more relaxed outlook with fewer money worries and a somewhat more affluent life style. While visiting and interviewing retired and older persons in New England, I happened upon one of those rare cases where the answers were so simple and frank, and the logic so clear, I had to capture the "Katzenjammer Kid" plan, every last detail. Let me share with you the Nobby Anderson method.

My wife and daughter had been traveling with me and we had come to one of those irresistible New England gift shops, and naturally the ladies had to check it out. I very quickly had my fill and was idling near our car, when I noticed this man looking at me, and he seemed friendly and anxious to talk.

*He told me he had retired early, at age fifty-eight and I said
we were birds of a feather since I had checked out at fifty-nine. He
grew chatty, and I smelled a very practical and usable experience
story. So I asked if he would tell everything, his whole life-and-
work saga; and here it is:*

"You have to understand," he said, "that I never expected to
amount to very much. We were a big family, and poor. I don't really know if we were all that poor, but we were not very happy at
our house. My old man was pretty tough; and when I say he
always grabbed the biggest piece of meat or pie, I mean that's
what he really did. I was anxious to get out of there as soon as I
could. Left when I was fifteen, been making my way ever since.

"Along the way, I got married. My wife is pretty much the
same kind of folks I came from—poor and uncertain, scared
mostly. We were not sure we could make it, but damn sure we
couldn't stand to make many fool mistakes. I got a job as sort of a
tool and die maker, and worked my way up with that skill.
Worked in a small shop in a small town, only from ten to twenty
workers there.

"Nice old guy ran the place and he was mostly good to us.
Some times were tough and we didn't get raises for several years,
just glad to keep our jobs. Some years the old man came around
and gave each old-timer a share of stock in the company instead
of a raise. Now, what the devil was I to do with a share of stock
in his company*—kept them though. We couldn't eat that, nor put
it in the bank either. Hung on to it, and over the years, I got a
number of them*—once again, instead of more money.

"My wife and I did what we could to get ahead. We'd buy
some little old house, fix it up, and maybe sell it; then we did it
again. And sometimes we kept them, to rent out. We ended up,
over the years, with a number of modest properties which brought
in a little rental income; and it worked because I could do all the
fixing myself.

"But, one day, the old man called us all together and there
were his two sons sitting alongside of him. Those kids never were
any good around the place; never saw them much; off to school
and stuff like that. But here they all were and you could sure smell

*what was coming up next. The old man told us he was tired out,
not too well, and he was going to retire; the boys would be taking
over.*

*"You know, it didn't take very long before those young fel-
lows had five or six of us older guys on the way out—out of a job.
Told you I always figured I was never going to amount to much."*

*Watching Nobby Anderson closely, I noticed the slightest
withering to his arm, and I thought I saw a touch of a limp on one
side. He was an odd little man, somewhat shy and yet common
sense smart; a bit suspicious, perhaps, but friendly enough with
me during our visit. I suspected he had to tell his story to someone. He looked like one of those people who expect to be dealt
poor cards in life's game; and one wonders if that is another self-
fulfilling prophesy.*

*"What did you do then, Mr. Anderson; where did you find
work?" "I finally got a job as sort of a traffic shipping guy in a
small chemical company. Took a while, but I did end up working
there almost ten years. That company was taken over by a bigger
chemical outfit, and you know how those mergers work. Nothing's
going to change, same crew and all, and then they come snooping
around and pretty soon they're changing everything. Same old
crap."*

*"What came next; what did you do them?" We both smiled,
he with a shrug. His face was without much expression, without
trace of enthusiasm or self-pity.*

*"Well, I was pushin' toward my sixties, then, and I figured it
was getting too late to start over; too tough to get anywhere.
Decided to sit down and figure it all out. Did plenty of thinking
and planning, the wife and me, we worked it out. I wasn't on
social security, not yet, though I'll get there, will be sixty-three
soon and I'm going to take it. But, like I'm telling you, that was
about four or five years ago when that last job went down the
drain. Mind you, I ain't complaining. Never expected to amount
to much anyway, so I guess I didn't miss my not getting there. Retired now, and enjoying it okay."*

*Anderson told me how they looked around for a place to
live—near a mountain, not too far from the sea so they could
drive there in a day or less, and close enough to run into Boston*

or even New York if they had a mind to. They come and go when they want. He said, "We don't live big, but we live alright."

Finally, I explained to Nobby Anderson my research role, and asked, even though we were strangers, if he would tell how they managed—the money and everything. And he did, without much pause at all.

"Like I said, Sir, I never expected to amount to much, you know, in money and work and all, so we hung onto everything. Bought more houses, fixed them, sold some, kept some to rent out. Picked up a few bucks—put some of that money into some stocks, got burned a few times, and got mighty careful. Couldn't risk those losses. We sold out a while back, guess we got out just in time, made a little too. Market's been down all these years since. For once, we were one of the smart ones—or lucky."

He explained in country talk about greed, "When your pail's full is a good time to take it away from the cow—before she kicks it all down the gutter."

"We ended up, all told, with $136,000," Anderson explained.

Whether you and I think that a lot or a little, doesn't matter. We can add or subtract our own zeros, move around our own decimal points. But this was the story of one man's experience—how he harnessed his assets to his simple expectations, how he mixed fears, worries, and caution with some guts, and how he ended up winning at least part of the game.

"First thing we did with that $136,000 was to spend $40,000 on a very fine, very old, pegged-plank floor, farm home nestled up against the sheltered side of a small mountain in Vermont. That's where we live now; beautiful view with the sunrise peeking in one side in the morning, and the setting sun sliding in the valley in the west, in the evening. I tell you, it's some home."

"You mean you dropped forty thousand bucks out of that hundred and thirty six thousand into a house? You can't eat a house; and anyway, isn't that too much money to sink in a house

*at this stage of your life?'' I challenged Anderson. He simply
smiled, with more poise than I expected of him.*

*"Remember, we still had $96,000 left in assets, our modest
investments—we've got income. Those shares of stock the old
man gave us, well, they were bought back by his boys and that
gave me about $10,000. And then that chemical company had a
profit-sharing deal, and in ten years, that amounted to a good
little bit. And now I'm fixing to go on social security. That all
adds up to a fair income.*

*"First thing, after buying that house, I started to pay myself
$1,000 per month, and that's $12,000 per year the way I figure.
All my life I worked for other people; now I work for me.''*

*I asked Nobby Anderson what the remaining $96,000 paid
him each year.*

*"It's running about $9,000 now.'' Anderson saw my eye-
brows raise up, and he continued, "I know, I'm paying us $12
grand and taking in only $9 grand—at this time. But you've got to
remember, I'm very handy. My wife and me, we take off, go
where we please, and sometimes I pick up things to do, here and
there. Usually pick up another $2,000 a year. I know we are
$1,000 short each year, but just for a little longer. Then, very
soon, I'm going on social security, and I can stop doing those odd
job things.*

*"Besides, I don't mind running just a little short for a while,
because when we get that $96,000 down to $60,000 by eating
away at our principal, then we're going to buy two $15,000 single
premium annuities and that'll give us another $200 per month.
With that, and all the rest, we are going to be able to live forever.''*

*"Mr. Anderson, you had best be careful, or you might end
up, as you say, 'not amounting to very much,' all over again!''*

*Now he smiled a bit patronizingly, I thought, and then he
chided me, "You, Sir, worry too much. I have this all worked out
on twenty-year charts. We all live a long time in this mean old
family, some to high eighties and even ninety. But I have it all
factored out, and as I say, with everything we'll have a couple
hundred from those annuities (when we get down that far) and
we'll get another couple hundred from social security. And with*

that plus all the rest, we will be able to go on living until we die, and that's got to be a long way off for us. We are having a good life, finally. I guess I didn't really retire, just changed bosses. I don't happen to think that what we're doing is any big deal, it's just plain common horse sense, and that's plenty necessary at our house since we never could risk no damn fool surprises. But, now I'm the boss, and I'm about the best one I ever had.''

I shook my head at Nobby Anderson's tale, and then I shook his hand and told him how much his very elemental factoring made sense, if it works as he told me. He suggested I work it all out on paper when I got home, and I have done that, with Nobby Anderson's figures, and then with our own. It does work.

On the following chart, fill in the income expected and on the next chart the income needed. You will find that we are acknowledging the continuing inflationary trend and have suggested that this also be built in—on both charts—inflation on the income needs chart and indexing and appreciation on the income chart. In any event, this thirteen-year chart (from age sixty-five to age seventy-eight will help you to factor out and to dramatize where it's all going and what you will be needing—what you might have to do to plug up any holes, to sell off assets or to buy any of a number of kinds of income-producing vehicles, or whatever. To make the filling-in of the following chart materials easier, refer back to chapter 3, to the income and money-needs charts, and draw from them the *annual* figures you will want to assemble here, for guidance in projecting income, and income need, to age seventy-seven, and beyond.

Your Annual Income Expectation (from all possible sources). Build in all sensible appreciation and indexing estimates. *For example,* **add 10 percent for appreciation,** *each year,* **on real and other property.** **Add from 5 to 7 percent for any indexing**

Project your annual expected income from your age, individual or family income.

Amount Expected—Year Due to be received	65th, 19__	66th, 19__	67th, 19__	68th, 19__	69th, 19__
	$	$	$	$	$
Social Security SSI: supplemental SS Pension fund payment Profit-Sharing payout Deferred income; Other:					
Annuity payments Disability payments Any other guaranteed income sources:					
Any earned incomes Settlement fees, etc.					
Rental income expected Royalties; Licensing Any other fees, etc.					
Sales of collectibles Buying or selling (Real or other property; Property disposed of)					
Inheritance income Alimony payments Dependency income					
Investment income Government issues Bonds Stocks (list them)					
Other interest due Other dividends due					
TOTAL BY YEARS	$	$	$	$	$

such as cost-of-living upward adjustments on Social Security, pensions, etc.

70th, 19__	71st, 19__	72nd, 19__	73rd, 19__	74th, 19__	75th, 19__	76th, 19__	77th, 19__
$	$	$	$	$	$	$	$
$	$	$	$	$	$	$	$

Your Annual Income Needs (for all living purposes). Be sure to build in a sufficient inflation factor. For example, you may be wise to add, on average, as much as 7 or

Project your annual income needs from your age, for individual or family needs.

Amount Needed—Year Income Needed:	65th, 19—	66th, 19—	67th, 19—	68th, 19—	69th, 19—
Food, regular Food, entertaining Housing, rents or mortgage payments Costs of auto	$	$	$	$	$

Costs for gasoline
Other transportation
Health insurance
  Medicare
  Supplemental coverage					

Other health care Clothing, purchases Clothing, maintenance Recreational costs Vacation trips					

Home, maintenance
Home, furnishings
Church and charities
Personal needs
Financial expenses or
  savings set aside
  Insurance payments
  Interest payments
  Loan payments
  Taxes to be paid,
    Income Taxes,
    Real estate taxes,
    Gift taxes due					

Support payments Any other expenses					

Purchases, New auto
  Second home
  Boat or other RV					

Contingency, expected
  or unexpected
Being-Nice-to-You,
  Special trips
  or other treats					

TOTAL BY YEARS	$	$	$	$	$

8 percent for inflationary increases. (Later you can match inflation's increase against indexing and cost-of-living adjustment factors.)

70th, 19__	71st, 19__	72nd, 19__	73rd, 19__	74th, 19__	75th, 19__	76th, 19__	77th, 19__
$	$	$	$	$	$	$	$
$	$	$	$	$	$	$	$

The *Minneapolis Tribune* runs countless upbeat articles, and a recent one quoted five executives from various sections of the financial community, and their views about "What do you do with a nest egg?" All of these experts noted that age, expectation of future income, size of family, and similar factors would influence their advice to a given individual. These advisers were counseling, in the newspaper, about smaller nest eggs, and were suggesting a conservative way to go. They advise security of corpus, and income, to yield *the highest safe income*. A recent issue of *Better Homes and Gardens,* certainly the voice of prudence to millions of mid-Americans, featured a substantial article entitled, "How Long Will Your Nest Egg Last?" Generally, this piece, which was apparently written with the guidance of Virginia Forsythe and Barbara Quint, uses the hypothetical nest egg corpus of $50,000, and this is as good a figure as any. They cover essentially the same data we have been examining—the life expectancy tables and their significance in these calculations. Their charts show percent of capital you may safely withdraw annually, if your money is invested at the indicated percentages of interest. Basically, this article's examination suggests three overall criteria: 1) Lock in some money forever. That is, for specific inheritance arrangement. 2) Spend extra money now to enjoy suppressed desires while you still have the spirit, the stamina, and especially, *the legs* to negotiate all those stairs, hilly walkways and byways. The writers show how to do it all safely, using the doubling of your life expectancy method, until, as they say, "the principal would be depleted." And 3) Spread it all out, using some of it now, and the rest factored for living use, for as long as the years of your life expectancy.

Even the responsible and conservative publications of the American Association for Retired Persons present such encouragement to be examined and considered by their many millions of members, many of whom are not very comfortable with any ideas about eating your seed corn, of ever being tempted to even touch principal and corpora. One such article in *Dynamic Maturity* (now *Dynamic Years,* which is the member organ of A.I.M., Action for Independent Maturity), the younger crowd of the AARP, was entitled "Their Aim Is to End Up Broke." This is the carefully considered intent of the Colin family in California who know just what they want to do with their retirement savings—they are planning to "spend every penny of it." With carefully worked out cost and income charts, the Colins convinced the

writer, Elliot Carlson, not only of their wish, but their specific intent
to live this way. But as they conclude the article, they do have this
hedge.

> *"Of course, the Colins know that tougher times may come. In an
> emergency, they could easily get $40,000 for their twenty-year-
> old house, for which they paid $18,000 in 1958; they could buy a
> mobile home for $15,000, and use the rest to generate more
> retirement income. But they hope they'll never need to do this.
> They like their home, the garden and the patio, surrounded by
> peach and nectarine trees and a vine-covered wall. In fact, the
> Colins say they would bê happy if they ended their lives with
> nothing more to their names than the house.*

Take your pick of all of the available ways to make your life's
economic progress serve your needs in your later years—whether to
draw it down so you can live it up, or whether to factor in some principal to enrich your retirement and later years. The ball is, as they say
in the gentler sports, "in your court."

> *Bernard Rummel was always a hardworking, skilled machine-tool
> specialist. After working for years for others, he started a shop of
> his own. And, as the years went by and Bernard's work quality
> and service reputation grew, so did his business volume. Time
> passes, and we grow older and wearier, and so did Bernard Rum-
> mel. Everything was always used to expand and build the business
> so that Rummel never took more than $17,500 out of the business
> in any one year (and that may have been a pretty good salary,
> until a few years ago, for a man who had always been paid by
> others).*
>
> *After the kids were grown and gone, Harriet helped Bernard
> with his correspondence, his accounts receivable, and the books;
> but she also continued with part-time employment, outside of the
> business, to help out. She never earned more than $3,000 in any
> one year, and therefore, the Rummels had income, together, of
> about $20,000 annually (this included any profit Bernard took
> from the business). Naturally with these cautious methods, the
> business grew in volume and worth.*
>
> *By and by, the Rummels came to the brink of their retirement*

*years, without really having all of their business things properly
organized. A buyer appeared, and though the business had not
been for sale, Bernard Rummel took what seemed to him a more
than generous offer. Then they discovered a new problem—
besides the income tax.*

*Harriet had minimal social security, but Bernard's was near
the maximum; he had been advised, and had set up a pension program so that they would now have this income. There had been
business profits, and that which had not been plowed back for
growth had simply gone into certificates of deposit, and had accumulated without much notice.*

*The business was purchased by a combine, which included a
few of his most talented younger associates. This was accomplished with the help of a sound local bank, on a modified
land contract which served both buyer and seller advantageously.*

*It seemed to have turned out to be a good deal for all, except
that now, the Rummels have annual income—from their own benefit income, all those certificates, plus the annual installment-plus-
interest—of more than double any annual income they ever had,
or even imagined. They had both reached their very early seven-
ties, and since they had always been such hard workers, and such
careful managers and savers, they were quite without experience
at spending money, having good times, or living it up. They had
the money, and it would keep coming for as long as they lived—
and from the business, for much longer than that. But they did not
have the knowledge, or the comfortable experience, of how to
enrich their lives. Not that their lives had lacked richness—they
were successful and well respected. They only lacked flair to go
along with their extremely good fortune.*

What connection has the Rummel experience with the principle of
whether or not to use up principal—a theory and practice which fasci-
nates some and alarms many? And who can say which among the universe of successes and failures ought or ought not to toy with this old-
time mortal sin of economic behavior?

What adds relevance to the Rummels' story of hard working
growth and great good fortune, is that just last month I spotted this
obituary:

Bernard Rummel, age seventy-two, died unexpectedly, in the same community where he and Harriet had always lived, and worked, and succeeded.

Perhaps, that is all that we can ask of life. I wish that I could visit with Bernard once again to ask him (how) what else—if anything—he might have managed differently. It might be that he and Harriet already had so much more than they had every conceived possible, and maybe that is enough.

6

Retire Richer: Earn Mini-Career Money

No one lives content with his condition, whether reason gave it to him, or chance threw it his way.

HORACE:
Satires

Retirement, whether we like it or not, will arrive at our house, some day in some way, either when *we* decide, or when *they* dictate. There appears to be a great unevenness in the grace with which each of us accepts this inevitable reality.

There has been a lot of fussing about mandatory retirement—whether it be just, foolish and unfair, or wasteful of still useful human resources. I consider the question academic. I am neither for it nor against it, but find it part of the inevitable condition whereby both labor and management keep cleaning out the work force. Besides, *over half of all workers* take their social security at age sixty-two; and 60 percent are already on social security by the time they reach sixty-five. There is in this fact strong evidence that the people are opting to "jump ship early." Apparently, an increasing number either wish to stop what they are doing, or they hope to try something new with the years that are left for them—that generation of "free time." These are the bonus years in which many prefer to freshly fulfill themselves at new tasks, in new places, with new people, and under the new and more relaxed condition of their retirement years.

The real trick seems to be to have something lined up that we wish to do, especially early in our retirement years. I am repeatedly warned to remind my audiences that most of us will need "some kind of a bridge" to get us from the regimented and structured work systems of our lives into that freedom land, where we have to make our own decisions about what we are going to do—or not do—with our newly abundant free time.

The regimen under which we live during our working lifetime is a great deal easier to handle, many retirees are finding, than all that free choice of time which gets dumped on them, apparently as a near total surprise. There is a comforting structure to the nature of career jobs. We know where we have to be, what time we must be there, what we are expected to do, and, most of the time, how we are expected to do it. If we lapse in any of these, we are reminded what is expected of us. True, we work hard, but we are free of all that activity decision-making, since there is such a familiar framework around our working days and our tasks.

And then we come to retirement. Now we are free to do anything, but we don't know quite how to begin unless we have done constructive planning. This is why many find that new activity, perhaps a new part-time job, provides at least a partially structured replacement for all those comfortable habits of our career assignments.

Dr. Kurt Dietzler, Ph.D., a teacher and preacher from Marburg, Germany, wrote his doctoral dissertation on the subject of preretirement planning and preparation. He explained to me an experiment they had conducted, both at Marburg and at Heidelburg Universities, whereby young people, at the very beginning of their career jobs, were given a course of instruction about planning for their retirement. On the face of it, I thought that age ridiculously early. But he assures me—and cautions American education to keep an open mind on this subject—that once young people get involved in such a course, they take a great deal of interest in charting their entire working lives toward a goal which encourages hopes, dreams, and ambitions, rather than what seem to be such unrewarding and surprising shocks of retirement, as too often viewed by American workers. Unfortunately, too many miss the happy point about the reward for a "job well done," and instead concentrate on the feelings of being dumped, useless, of having been emasculated and in the way.

Sylvia Porter, the very practical economic columnist, wrote a piece recently under the title "The 20s, the Right Age to Plan for the Future." Among other sensible comments, she pointed out that early attention to our postemployment years may be the only way we can do the best job of planning for pension and other benefit alternatives. That by starting early we get involved in the *wonderful magic of compound interest* which seems to need only an early beginning and a long time to multiply increasingly and favorably.

One of the nicer and most rewarding aspects of your retirement is that you will finally have the time for the things you "never had time to get around to before." But I must warn you that none of this will happen automatically. You will have to make it all happen. And let us not get too involved with all those restrictive attitudes like, "but we can only earn so much (or so little) before they penalize us by taking away part of our social security." That had been a fact, and still is, in part. But, beginning in 1978, the annual earnings test has been changed to permit individuals of sixty-five and over to earn up to $4,000 per year without losing any benefits. Individuals who are younger may earn up to $3,240. Both figures will increase in subsequent years, with separate tests continuing to apply separately to both age categories. In both cases, earnings above the allowable limit will result in a deduction of $1 in benefits for each $2 earned over the limit. Over the next several years, there will also be a progressive increase in what may be earned without any loss of benefits.

But, if you wish to make some fresh new money in some fresh new way, and if this is the only way you can get that new income, *after your earnings limitations* have been reached, then you must decide if you are willing to work for those fifty-cent dollars.

You might be willing, if you like what you would be doing, if you would rather be doing it than not, if you find fulfillment and new importance in what you would be doing.

Security was once a very comforting word. Security was freedom from anxiety and doubt; it implied a feeling and assurance of safety and certainty. But times have changed, and security means many more (or perhaps, many less) things now—for example, the hollow promise of our own so-called "security blanket concepts." Today, if security does not strongly exist in your heart and spirit, and in your gut, it probably does not exist at all—for you.

It may be in order now, to consider *preparing* for your retirement. There are an increasing number of very good seminars and workshops, adult courses of learning, through which the worker can discover the problems and opportunities about one's pending retirement in a classroom and workshop atmosphere. Communicating with the other workers and spouses in these classes makes for a great deal of sharing of hopes, dreams, and concerns about this new condition. There are church groups and insurance organizations which are mounting such training sessions. The community colleges, some of the universities, and technical training schools have evening classes for individuals and couples. The younger division of AARP, A.I.M., (Action for Independent Maturity) has an excellent course which they make available through organizations and companies. Those who have attended report that it comes to grips with the big questions and provides at least some of the answers, and encourages them to keep working on the project toward their own retirement. Not just training for retirement as an end, but learning how to look ahead into our later years with the full expectation that we are going to enjoy retirement living and the freedom to "do something we've always wanted to do."

How Some Retired Richer: To Earn Mini-Career Money*

Ted Calhoun retired early because of his wife's health. He took her South, to Houston, Texas, where they were overwhelmed by the vastness of everything. Buildings, space, everything was so big and so high: high-rise buildings and high-price everything. Ted had to find something to do, to keep busy and to earn extra money to help and to pay for this new higher cost living.

Back home in the woodsy North, in Wisconsin, Ted had worked at logging, roofing houses, pumping gas, and fixing cars. Ted Calhoun knew how to fix anything. So that is what the Calhouns had printed on 500 business cards, which they stuffed

---

*From "Retire Richer: Earn Mini-Career Money" by Elmer Otte, Courtesy of Field Newspaper Syndicate, 1976, Field Enterprises, Inc.

under doors and stuck behind mail boxes at homes in Houston residential areas:

Ted's Fix-It Service
Ted Can Fix Anything
$5.00 per hour
Phone: 220-6707
for free estimates

The Calhouns had so many calls asking for free estimates that he had too little time to fix anything, and thus to earn extra new income. Next time around, they had 500 more cards printed, but this time they left off mention of free estimates. They slid these cards under apartmvent doors because that was more efficient, with less driving around. Now Ted is busy fixing things and they are enjoying sufficient extra income. He works when and as much as he wants to.

Some retirees protest that they do not want to work after they retire. "If I have to get a retirement job, I may as well not retire." Good point, except that most do not have a choice. You are going to be retired, either when they dictate or when you decide. Earning new money—especially at something new and different—when we want to work, adds zest to retirement. Such extra income makes us feel we are still useful, still important; and, nothing fights inflation and budget-busting costs any better.

Ziggy Peterson has enough money for a nice retirement. His wife has even more. But Ziggy is a collector, from auction goodies to garage sale stuff. He also likes to collect still more new money. "Snowbird" neighbors in his Phoenix suburb employ Ziggy to check on their Arizona places while they fly north for the summer. They pay him from ten to twenty dollars a month–cash. Most days, Ziggy and his little dog companion make their security rounds, earning what he calls "walking-around money."

Surprising numbers of retirees, faced with longstanding financial fears, are later surprised when they keep accumulating new money.

Orin Talcot retired from the Methodist ministry in Indiana. On one of his first free days, he visited an old preacher friend and discovered beekeeping. Now, Orin has two dozen hives of honey bees which he enjoys tending. He harvests old-fashioned comb honey. Mrs. Talcot is delighted with Orin's new fascination, because she had feared he might be pining for the old pulpit days. She hopes they will eventually pick up some new honey money, "if I can ever get Orin to stop giving the honey away to his many friends."

What skills do you have left over? Have you a marketable hobby? Is there anything you can make and sell? What about your collections? (Almost everyone hangs onto something, much of it sought after and saleable today.) There could be new fun and extra money for you, in buying, selling, and trading any type of collectibles which excite your interest.

Sid Hillman tunes pianos in his retirement. He says there is a shortage of piano tuners and an abundance of out-of-tune pianos. Tuning them is easy to learn: from systems taught by mail, from experienced individuals, or even from courses at some colleges. Sid says he works when he wants to and only as much as he wishes. The extra cash Sid earns ($15 to $50 per piano) makes sweet music in his retirement pocket.

Go home-hunting in any of those attractive retirement communities along the mid-Atlantic, in Arizona, California, Florida, or anywhere. Who do you suppose drives folks around in those mini-buses? Those are other retired persons, people who like to be with people. They show and tell, and some of them also sell. And, they get paid for this pleasant, part-time work.

George Paxton retired from farming in upper New York state. Now, he owns two homes near a popular retirement area in Florida. The Paxtons rent out one and live in the other. George has a part-time job he enjoys. Mornings, he is the golf-cart jockey at a busy country club nearby. Keeping those carts ready and in top condition is duck soup for this retired farmer; he knows equip-

ment and how to keep it running. George is happy to be busy and outdoors, and his wife is delighted to have him out of the house, and not underfoot.

The biggest concern about earning extra income in retirement is losing social security benefits. At present, (1978) any retired sixty-five-year old person may earn up to $4,000 per year and still get full social security benefits. This is called the "annual earnings test." Beyond the above amounts, it takes two earned dollars to net one benefit dollar.

Pete Hanson beat the system. His career job involved buying seasonal shoe inventories for his employer's discount store chain. When Pete retired, he took a mini-job selling those same shoe lines for one of the companies he formerly bought from. Now he sells them to companies like his former firm. He earns high commissions and still draws some social security besides.

Is there buying or selling in your retirement future? Check this list of idea-starters, which suggests activities retired persons can harness to turn free time into extra income:

- How about being a sales person in discount stores, shopping centers, for real estate selling, or representing home needs products?
- Can you strum a banjo, blow a horn, bang the drums in supper club combos? Play the piano and sing at piano bars?
- Cater parties, tend bar, prepare fancy dishes, be a paid host?
- Repair and service small engines, and fix whatever they power?
- Use your imagination, look around, ask questions, volunteer. Avoid investing saved money, signing contracts, risking too much!

Could you be a self-employed person? What would you really like to try doing, to earn added money, and to bring fulfilling activity to abundant leisure hours?

Before you leap into social security problems, however, or into any of the retirement sucker traps which are set all around, do your homework carefully. Investigate, ask questions, seek advice and counsel. And move slowly. What you do not need now is a brand new retirement headache.

Finally, sit down and contemplate. "Why am I doing all of this? Do I really want to be the richest guy at my own funeral?" Do whatever you do for fun, or for love, *and then do it* for a bit of extra life-sweetening cash. Do it to enrich retirement, not to sour it. And, promise yourself to enjoy the activity and the challenge, even more than the money. Will you be able to sell your skills, or your hobby or other interests; and how will you go about it? Retirement is a wonderful opportunity for many to cash in on the experiences of their lives, and here are some of the ways to go about doing it. One good first step to take is to convince yourself that there is hope for you to do things that have meaning for you—activities which satisfy your creative or collecting skills, for example, things which might very easily turn into extra money. Let's look at a few examples:

Jon McMasters loves to carve wood. He carves wooden birds, small animals of all kinds, he even makes miniature bird houses. He gives many of these away to friends and family; but Jon also has begun turning out quantities of these items, and gift shops in his area snap them up. They are not costly; they are not large; but they are in delightfully good taste, and the workmanship is of a very high quality. Jon McMasters' creativity is paying off in two ways: he has activity he enjoys, and the products he turns out have created their own demand and income.

At Shell Point Village near the Sanibel Bridge at Fort Myers, Florida, I met a retired college teacher from New York state, who was in charge of a large section of their crafts programs, weaving, doll-work, stitchery, and the like. This pleasant retiree had exchanged her busy college career for a home for her aging years. She is eighty-four. She says she is all alone in the world, and wanted to come to a place like Shell Point Village because it had a connection with the church of her faith; and it also provided for lifetime health care once she got there. She told the folks at Shell Point Village she'd love to come if she could bring her loom and they promptly embraced her. Now she is really quite busy, happily busy, in charge of those crafts which were her career specialty. Now in her fulfilling and happy retirement, and on a

*much less demanding scale, she does pretty much as she has al-
ways done in her professional working life; and she does it for
appreciative, and eager-to-learn residents and friends from the
community which is now her home. Because she happened to be
ready to capitalize on the opportunity when it came, she looks
forward to a happy lifetime of doing exactly what she likes to do
best; and doing it with others, new neighbors and new friends.
People very much like herself.*

*I was visiting an old aunt in one of those professional nursing
homes recently when we were interrupted by a very gallant En-
glish gentleman who rapped, entered, and said, "Some mail for
you, my dear." Now it happens that my old aunt has not been
greeted in this fashion during very much of her long lifetime, but
you should have seen good old Aunt Jo smiling broadly.*

*The old gentleman turned toward me and wanted me to guess
his age. I said that I thought it was somewhere between eighty
and one hundred and he said, "You're not even trying, you're not
close. I am ninety-nine, Sir. My name is Malcolm MacDougal and
I am a Scot. I am delighted to be at this place and I am especially
delighted to have this wonderful job of delivering the mail to each
of my friends in each of the rooms of this home."*

He gets no pay, he hadn't even been asked to do this task; but he
gets a huge psychological reward. He meets and makes so many new
friends; he brings so much good cheer to this otherwise, often cheer-
less place. Opportunity is where we find it—rather, it is where we
look, and then discover it for ourselves.

*Carroll Hilton is a retired sales manager, retired at age sixty-two
from two back-to-back careers with paper and packaging companies. Carroll loves to go fishing, likes traveling, and walking on
sunny beaches. Every afternoon he goes swimming at an indoor
pool in his four-seasons area. But Carroll does something else
which fills his need for activity and uses some of his life's skills
and interests. And for Carroll, all of this has turned into a pleasant money tree.*

*He markets ready-to-plant, ready-to-grow trees. He calls
them fresh-air machines and uses clever and effective marketing*

techniques which work well and profitably for him. He sells these trees direct from the nursery, when they're about two feet tall, in quantities of several hundred or several thousand to companies which use them for opening events, as open-house giveaways, or as customer premiums. Others use them for seasonal promotions which fit their business, such as paper companies and packaging firms with which Carroll has long been familiar.

All of his work in this specialized business boils down to about three months activity. In the fall and winter he fusses about the promotional campaign he will use to stir up next year's sales volume (some of it will be repeat business) and then he follows up leads by telephone, and in person. He wraps up a satisfying volume of business—which keeps Carroll and his business-minded wife busy and active—taking in enough extra income to provide an annual European trip and a couple of months on the sunny beaches of the South.

Each year Carroll wonders if he should do it again; if he should bother once more; but each year the sweet smell of that reasonably automatic money tree is too much to resist and he goes at it, for one more time. He has pleasant activity and personal fulfillment. Carroll has never been able to successfully resist the lure of that extra cash. And why should he?

Most well organized and well run retirement communities are long on activities and facilities. They have classrooms, halls, and studios, with workshops on end where both men and women work at silversmithing, jewelry-making, sewing, knitting, stitchery, needlepoint, woodworking, and heaven knows what else. They repair toys and make new ones. They make things to sell, have regular, ongoing sales programs, as well as exhibitions and salons, to which people come to shop and buy gifts. A lot of retirement time is absorbed in fascinating ways by interesting and talented people in these wonderfully equipped facilities, which are one of the finest blessings for so many of these energetic folks who don't want to sit down and quit—not just yet. There is a camaraderie here and a pride, an ambition to take on new and tougher assignments. There may be many people who would rather go off sightseeing, but I notice many of these craftspeople also get in plenty of sightseeing. In the process, they pick up native materials and ideas and come back to their workshops refreshed and newly excited to take on even more challenging creative tasks.

Often doctors, managers, and other professional people come to their retirement, or to the opportunity to retire early, and it changes the direction of their lives.

For example, I have a doctor acquaintance, who specialized in family practice and surgery. He has just left his practice to go into a new kind of photographic essay development in one of the larger metropolitan communities, near where there are better facilities and a better market for this idea. Apparently, this doctor had been a hobby photographer for a long time, and became a serious student of the development of slide stories and photo essays. Now he feels the need to become more expert in this newly unfolding field.

Another physician in Missouri left his profession and became a resident sales and service expert in a shopping center, where he guides buyers in their selection of camera, film development equipment, and materials, based on his personal knowledge from his lifetime hobby of photographer, developer, and film printer.

Any supermarket discount operator would give his eyeteeth to find persons this dedicated, devoted and knowledgeable, to help customers make intelligent purchases in this and many other such complex and costly fields.

Ellie and Norman Nelson were in one of the workshop sessions I formerly directed in an adult vocation school. He had been a tool-and-die designer, and she worked in retail sales. They wanted to retire when he was fifty-five and she would still be fifty-one, and they hoped to travel, for at least six months of the year, on the European continent. One day we were working together which collective skills they might turn into money-makers, but I noticed they weren't paying much attention. There was a reason, and Norman was quick to elaborate. He "gave me hell" for suggesting, and guiding them into, activities for new work so that they could have extra money for this extra "living it up."

We had been gathering the facts of their retirement income,

*and he got upset because his financial situation was not quite as
rosy as he had hoped.* He gave me the devil because their money
wasn't adequate *for the joyful high-living they had in mind. He
said he was not interested in my trying to help him find ways to
pick up "extra chips" for all this extra living. I resisted reminding him that his plight was not of my doing. I never saw Ellie and
Norm Nelson again after that week-long session, but I often won-
dered whether they eventually turned their talents to useful and
productive activity to help flesh out their inadequate retirement income.*

*On the other hand, a Navy buddy from World War II put
together about the best preretirement income plan I ever heard
about. He stayed in the Naval Reserve for twenty years to pick up
a partial pension, beginning at age sixty. These part-time Naval
Reserve training sessions were one day a week, and also included
a week-long summer cruise and training mission. He completed
his job career in the postal service at age fifty-five, and was able
to retire from there with a pension based on thirty years of service.*

*Good old Alex completed these two public service careers,
and then picked up a new half-day part-time job, which earned his
social security rights,* and *gave him activity time and a sufficient
new income. He said that he received more income from that half-
day's effort than he had ever gotten from his postal work.*

*But there is more to Alex's story. His wife had also worked, first
in a department store where she had qualified under social security, and later she joined the postal service so that she would
also be able to qualify for a partial pension. Finally they both retired permanently, at age sixty-two or so. They took with them, to
Florida, social security benefits for both of them, two pension
programs in his case, and one pension program in her case.*

*They had always been hardworking, prudent people, but both
also had other exciting interests. They traveled anywhere and everywhere enjoying, extensively, the cultures they discovered, the
people they met, and the new friends they made. All this had been
well beyond what was remotely possible during their long working
lifetimes. Alex and his spouse have been truly blessed with a loving family, with many friends, and with all these carefully man-*

aged programs providing the fuel and the purchasing power for their farflung activities and journeys.

The foregoing provides a clearer picture of how many people put together interesting ideas and activities which suit their talents and purposes.

7

Then Again— You May Remarry

I take thee . . . and thee . . . and thee . . .
"THE AMERICAN WAY OF MARRIAGE;
REMARRIAGE."
Look Magazine

Fifty percent of the couples living in one of the livelier retirement communities in Florida are "second-timers," according to a newsy bulletin from that inviting place.

"I don't believe it. I couldn't go through all that again, with still another man," was the aghast response from one of the women to whom this statistic was reported. She is still married, and her reaction may have been a Freudian commentary on her "then" attitude about her "then" husband.

To quote Dr. Joyce Brothers from *Good Housekeeping* magazine: "Evidence indicates that second marriages actually tend to be more successful than first marriages."

There is a growing kind of widowhood, the one which results from divorce. This reality might arrive much earlier, and if the divorcee does not remarry, his or her alone condition can last a long time. The unmarried state visits increasing numbers of seemingly secure persons of both sexes and it lasts for an increasing number of years for many.

Apparently, the decision is easily made to get married again, and some of these older guys and gals are just as inept, as any other age, at grabbing what is available—who is available—without enough research and study, without enough thoughtful consideration.

One such modern remarriage problem has to do with "what is his and what is hers," and how much of a right have the children who may come along into the remarried state, including those children who are older, and perhaps, involved in marriages of their own.

There are sensible, and self-protective, steps we can take: A young friend was marrying for the second time to a young man for whom this was the first trip to the altar. The clerk issuing the marriage license wanted to know if this couple had considered making out what she called a pre-nuptial agreement. Our young friend and her next husband had never heard of such precautionary paperwork and were not sure what good it would be—until they checked it out with an attorney. He worked out such an agreement—which did seem indicated in her case—because she had two small children from her first marriage; and there was also property still being divided between herself and the first husband. Further data about ante-nuptial agreements follows:

Pre- or Ante-nuptial Agreements

Marriage settlements are frequently desirable preliminaries to second or subsequent marriages, and they may sometimes be appropriate to first marriages when either the bride or groom already own substantial property. Ante-nuptial agreements do not sound very romantic perhaps, but, sooner or later they may facilitate and soothe family relationships. They can also prevent potential warfare among and with children or others who may hold claims to your property . . . or to his or her assets.

Take for example a marriage between a widower, aged sixty-two, and a widow, aged fifty-two. Each has substantial property and both have children. It helps to prevent misunderstandings if their ante-nuptial agreement provides that their individual properties will be kept separate . . . and upon the death of either spouse, will revert to his or her children. Such agreements should provide for a sufficient life estate for the survivor—if there is any question about the adequacy of the remaining property of either spouse to finance his or her customary standard of living, and to meet emergencies.

Husbands and wives in comfortable circumstances may not wish to have testamentary trusts in their wills. They may prefer to bequeath everything direct to each other, even though this method leads to higher taxes on the second death. But, each spouse may harbor one worrisome reservation. What if the survivor should remarry and leave a goodly portion, or even all, remaining property to a new wife or husband?

Such a dilemma might be solved by an agreement requiring that the survivor must keep in effect a will leaving to the children not less in value than half of what he or she (either survivor) possessed after distribution under the will of the first to die. And, if the total remaining at the time of the second death had shrunk to *less* than half, the children would receive it all. Such a document regarding a survivor's will, would assure the first to die that his or her half of the property would not later go off into strange channels.

Pre-nuptial agreements—however well-intended—can sometimes get in the way of romance. One Mr. Really Big we heard about got all tangled up in one—or tried to—and things are still unraveling. It seems he had a wife, plus a mistress of long standing. He also had the income to keep each, if not always happy, then at least in a comfortable style of separated living. The mistress grew impatient and pressured her keeper about getting into something more permanent, like marriage. But, he already had his wife.

Ultimately, he started divorce proceedings against his wife, and suggested to his mistress that they have a pre-nuptial agreement worked out between the parties, so that she would be looked after, but that his first wife would also be protected according to her longer tenure. Well, the mistress blew up, distressed, to put it mildly. So, the subject was dropped, and they eventually married and wife number one received the usual court-administered legal share of some property and some income.

Later, at Mr. Big's untimely death, it unfolded that he had suffered such guilt at what he had so long done to his loyal first wife, that he had willed the vast majority of his estate's worth to her—and left the mistress-wife without much, either in pre- or post-nuptial goodies.

Questions to Consider—Before Popping that Question Again

- After you have been widowed, or divorced, for a suitable amount of time, have you seriously considered staying unmarried? (Some

later-in-life singles report they enjoy a new freedom they never had before; and they cherish that.)
- What are the strongest reasons which cause you to consider remarriage? Are they economic? (It helps to be honest.) Are your reasons strongest on the need you have for companionship, for someone to look after, to love, and to be looked after by?
- Is the question before you because you have met someone you feel you can grow fond of, or are already fond of? Have you checked this candidate out with your head before your heart gets carried away?
- Will there be any problems with your children, with other family members, or close friends, if you should re-marry?
- Have you discussed, or do you know anything about, the other person's needs and wishes regarding sexuality? Are you sure you know your own mind about this essential ingredient?
- If you have assets, and if your candidate for re-marriage also has property, and income, have you considered, discussed, and arranged for, protective ante-nuptial arrangements?
- Do you know where you would live, after marrying again? His place, her place, some place else—maybe even far away? (Do you know what you, or the other party, would do about staying there, after one of you dies, or leaves for any other reason?)
- Finally, have you thought about what you would do—if this re marrying adventure should not work out?

It has often been accurately said that "a wise wife can be a wise widow." But, there is some homework to do, some looking ahead, some getting today's house in order so that tomorrow's house may be in better condition.

The one most vital preparation has to do with *how things are— and where they are:* It may not be easy (but it is far better now than later) for some wives to get some husbands to sit down and carefully spell out, and list, the factual details of:

- Health insurance, life insurance and annuity specifics.
- Retirement pension, and profit-sharing benefits.
- Invested assets; where they are held, who is handling on-going details; who has been making the decisions.

- Wills, trusts, other instruments which concern both partners, together and individually.
- Safe deposit boxes, joint or separate; are there others?
- Cash, or checking account and savings available for death-connected emergencies.
- Location of all agreements, policies, GI-connected discharge papers, insurance forms and policies, any disability papers, others.
- Any records, all of them, about *all* family members; his, hers, ours, theirs; whether from previous marriages which ended by death, divorce . . . or any other incumbrances.
- Who are your (family) advisors? Are there separate ones for you or for your spouse? Who are they; where located?
- Any chance the other spouse can begin to handle finances as part of the familiarization process? Why not?
- Do you both have separate savings, separate checking accounts— for unexpected events, emergencies?
- Are tax records, all pertinent data, easily available; who are your tax advisors?
- Updated location list of all persons, papers, details, you (either of you) will need; immediately at death of your spouse (Easier now; safer, and cheaper.)

I do not preach remarriage, nor advocate against it. My task is simply to witness what is happening; and what I see happening are many mistakes, but I also see a lot of lovely successes in the remarriage business.

Remarried widowed persons and divorcees often say: "We should all marry our second wives first, or our second husbands." That may be, but, another voice of experience insists: "We should make sure we don't marry the same sort of person twice."

Sorting Out the "Getting Married Again" Question:

	Yes:	No:	Maybe:
1. Have you considered the possibility of being married again?	___	___	___
2. Do you feel satisfied that you are ready to try marriage once again?	___	___	___

3. Have you thought about being alone for the rest of your life? ___ ___ ___
4. Do you know with some certainty which (staying alone or being married again) you would most prefer? ___ ___ ___
5. Are your children (if any) going to be involved in your decision? ___ ___ ___
6. Do you want them involved? ___ ___ ___
7. Are there other persons "with a vote?" ___ ___ ___
8. Are you clear in your own mind about your pro-and-con reasons about remarriage? ___ ___ ___
9. Do you find yourself looking at candidates? ___ ___ ___
10. Are you: too critical; or, not critical enough; are you afraid of misjudging? ___ ___ ___
   Comments:_____
   _____
11. Is there a romantic candidate in view? ___ ___ ___
12. Do you know your real "remarriage reasons?" ___ ___ ___
13. Are you suitably visible to get noticed? ___ ___ ___
14. Are you willing to work at better visibility? ___ ___ ___
15. Do you seek remarriage for economic reasons? ___ ___ ___
16. Do you seek love, and can you give it? ___ ___ ___
17. Is companionship one of the major factors? ___ ___ ___
18. Have you been internally honest about your views about sexuality if you marry again? ___ ___ ___

The need, or call it desire, for getting together apparently stems from many stimuli. She is a good cook, and he is a good eater, and in their early and innocent neighborliness they often pleased each other because "it is a joy to see a man who likes to eat"; and, "it is easy to appreciate a woman who can set a nice table. Besides it is not much fun eating alone—or living alone.''

> *"I'm going to Texas for three months this winter where I have this apartment waiting for me; and I don't like driving there all alone. It wouldn't cost anymore for the two of us than it would for just me; otherwise there you would be, back in the cold North; and don't we both need someone to go around with, to be with? So, why don't you just come with me—to Texas?''*

> *Gloria Hopkins had a very full and happy life with her first husband, Rudy. But, hard-working Rudy died and left Gloria, with adequate insurance, with little to do but get together with lady friends. In time, she had a call of commiseration from an old family friend, a preacher of her Church. They got together, had pleasant days re-kindling their old friendship–and as so often happens, they developed an insistent romance. But, the preacher had a wife who had been institutionalized for some time, and that was an obvious obstacle. Eventually, he received, from his bishop, permission (because of the nature of the wife's hopeless condition) to divorce her, and then to marry Gloria.*
> *Now Gloria and her new husband are busy making a happy second marriage, traveling abroad, both involved in his church activities, living a good new life together. The preacher's first wife has since died, and life goes on at the rectory.*

Having a spouse—being married and living with someone compatible—is one of the greatest possible assets we can have, to help us effect a successful adjustment to aging. But, the widowed state does arrive—*and this too often serves as an additional obstacle to old age.*

> *With just a touch of seriousness, and with a sprinkling of ample levity, I share this problem-solving suggestion–an idea that was once proposed, tongue-in-cheek, at a conference on aging where the widowed state was agenda number one. It was suggested, that since the majority of women end up widowed, and that further, there are too few men left over, to "go around," that perhaps a big business scheme might work: they called it "selling shares in Stanley.''*

Here is how it is supposed to work: four or five women, geographically scattered, would buy, or contribute to, "buying shares in Stanley," and this is what they would then do. By the seasons, Stanley would go to ersatz spouse, Melinda, in Vermont or New Hampshire, in the good old summertime. Comes the winter, Stanley would ship off to cruise around the Southeast, or the Southwest, with either Carol, or Millie, depending on whose time and turn it was. And, in between the seasons, busy Stanley would fly away to live still another life or two, in either the far Northwest, where Phyllis pined away for his return, or to the Midwest where Trudy would take time out from her alone life, to accommodate Stanley's visit there.

It is not clear whether this project would ever sell, but it does have fascinating potentials for "spreading the wealth" about.

Do not be bedeviled by the fiscal and legal aspects of getting married again; but permit an eyes-wide-open approach as it becomes adequately clear that getting one's fiduciary house in marrying order can, and may, have a great deal to do with—and to contribute toward—a once again happy married state.

The most secure way of fixing to inherit some of your own money, given the special circumstances of bringing together all those new parties, and all those segmented families, is by seeking sound advice on alternatives, and by following the very best of such advice. Then, getting married again may be really fun again. Felicitations to both of you, my dears.

8

Grandparents: Wasted Natural Resource

The people whom the sons and daughters find it hardest to understand are the fathers and mothers, but young people can get on very well with the grandfathers and grandmothers.
Ibid. CHAPTER 18
No Mean City.

Where have all the grandparents gone? They are not in our homes, not very often; and they are even less often companions to our children (their grandchildren). What a pity this is—for everyone! What a short-changing circumstance this is for all of society.

Grandparents stand even higher in the human values system than Boy Scouts or Girl Scouts. *They* are truly dependable, loyal, courteous and kind. If anyone has a no-vested-interest relationship, it is grandparents. Kids trust them. Kids have secrets with them; kids love them—if they *know* them at all. Grandparents have the greatest advantage in family structuring; parents are often adversaries—but grandparents are friends and colleagues.

Grandparenting is a two-edged opportunity. Everybody stands to benefit whenever grandparents are either permitted or encouraged to be participating members of families. And nobody loses. It may well be that the grandparents themselves are the greatest beneficiaries from their open and trusting relationships with grandchildren. It must be one of our saddest commentaries that those who most need an honest and open love and understanding—at both ends of family hierarchies—are staying so much, or are kept so much, apart.

142

*Angella Martines lives in Cleveland with her husband and family.
She told me, with a great and loving excitement, about her father
whom she claims is the most wonderful grandfather in the whole
world. This apparently delightful immigrant is friend and welcome
companion to all his grandchildren without regard to their ages
which run from six to twenty-six years. The little ones romp with
him and love him; and all of them, regardless of age, have many
happy visits together because this grandfather manages to live in
each of their worlds. He is not nosey, nor parenting; he is just a
very good friend.*

*Grandparents, Angella insists, have it all over parents.
Parents are more like the enemy. They are antagonists, frequently
on the other side of where the children most wish to be; opposites
on issues, on discipline and on point of view. Angella's father,
Grandpa Alfredo Martines, is none of these things. Not only is he
involved with his grandchildren, they take him along on their ex-
peditions. He is one of them. Of course, Grandpa Alfredo pays his
dues; not just by being a handy and cordial money tree for the
kids, but by being thoughtful of them and of all family members.
This wise, old-world patriarch must love all of his family very
much for he has made a "living gift" arrangement for every one
of them.*

*For the past ten years, Alfredo has provided two brand new
pairs of shoes for each of his grandchildren. He does the same for
his children; for each son, daughter or son-and-daughter-in-law.
Twice each year each grandkid, and each child or child-in-law,
may go shoe-shopping any time it pleases them. They may buy any
needed or desired pair of shoes, twice each year, and all they
have to do is bring the bill to Grandpa. No questions asked; no
quibble about the price, the style or the color. Just buy them and
wear them, and enjoy them.*

*But, no one who neglects to buy those two annual pairs of
shoes can ever get the money instead. It's shoes—two pairs of
shoes annually—or nothing.*

Research shows, that 70% of older people have living grandchildren. It is a sad fact that an alarmingly high percentage of these
grandparents and grandchildren do not see each other very often and

do not know each other very well. How *can* there be meaningful grandparent-grandchild relationships with the old folks increasingly living so separately and so far away? With all the racing-around mobility of today's young families, *that* twain shall seldom meet.

Booming retirement communities are just one example of this separation with their far away distance and the limits on time and frequency of grandchild visiting. One such segregated social segment, ironically located in the community of Young, Arizona, had a mighty hassle a year or two ago because one of the residents had permitted excessive visiting for some grandchildren.

For some years, in spring, summer and fall seasons, I watched a neighbor in his higher sixties holding Sunday morning dialogues with all of the little people from the neighborhood. Each Sunday they came to be with Morris on his patio, where he fed them cookies and milk and told them stories; all kinds of stories about people, places and fun things. Morris kept a warm but disciplined control over his little friends as they sat on stools, and blocks, and in coaster wagons, listening and talking with their friendly neighborhood philosopher. He was not really a teacher, just a friend to these little kids. None of the parents ever seemed to show any concern because they learned from their little ones what Morris shared with them. This unofficial "baby-sitting service" happened only on Sunday mornings when most of the parents and their older children were off at church. Of those who participated, I suspect that Morris got the most out of this relationship; he wasn't alone, he had a half dozen to a dozen friends depending upon him. Morris never talked much about his "Sunday school"—but he did smile about it; since these were principally Christian family children—and Morris was a respected Jewish neighbor; himself not a grandfather—except on Sunday mornings.

If grandparents are as smart as the smaller grandchildren think they are, as smart as grandparents have, for so long, been telling everyone they are, they ought to be able to find enough creative ways to harness some of their time and fascination in becoming a more vital part of the lives of their young heirs. Not just with money, or expensive gifts and favors, either. Some promising things *are* being done to bring some of the old in touch with some of the young.

As part of the Older Americans Act of 1971, there has been a project called the Foster Grandparents Program, which is federally-funded and conducted at the local level by The Area Office on Aging. This case in point quotes Rosemary Reginald, age 67, from out in the suburbs: "Where else are you gonna get a job where they kiss you?" Mrs. Reginald is a participant in the Foster Grandparents Program which is open to those of limited income over the age of sixty. It pays them a limited $1.25 an hour, plus carfare and lunch, for as many hours a day, as many days a week, as the "grandparent" can spare.

Too many older persons think they are too old to bother about anything any more. They spend too many days celebrating various health concerns and other negative aspects of aging. Doctors also err; too frequently they attribute curable conditions in older people to the aging process and thus fail to do anything about them. The need is to separate "how much is old from how much is sick," and then, to rigorously treat the sick.

Grandma O'Leary—and it does sound odd to call her grandma—doesn't seem to be any kind of stereotype in the grandmother business. She thinks nothing of piling a grandchild into her car in California and driving across the country to pick up another in the midwest, and to take both along with her to Maine for the summer. There they may be joined by still a few more of the Connecticut contingent of her grandchild universe. There is something special here: she doesn't just housemother and chauffer; she is more like one of them—enjoying with them.

One of her sons and his family have five children of scattered ages and they all took off for a three week trip throughout the far West. They picked up Grandma Madeline O'Leary and "did the West Coast together." With a motley collection of sleeping bags and other gear, they camped out, stayed at motels, and occasionally bedded down with relatives and friends. As the kids explained when they got back home, Grandma Madeline was more popcorn-eating-and-song-singing-fun than any of the kids. She was the one everyone wanted to be with and just about everybody said: "Boy, wouldn't it be neat to get to be a young grandma like Grandma O'Leary when we get old?"

There is a legend attached to the headboard of this grandma's bed, artfully lettered to read: "I'm not getting older

. . . I'm just living longer." And living is what this charming, smilingly cheerful, elegant, white-haired lady is doing just about all of the time. They say she's over 80, but I do not know how anyone could tell.

The guaranteed way to go unnoticed, unrecognized and unremembered, and therefore also unloved—in fact or in memory—is for you to leave them only your money, remembering them only in your codicils and trusts. It works far better if you bring some of it with you, if you come often while you are still a happy and living memory. Our own daughter-in-law is earnestly insistent that we come often and that we get to know each individual grandchild personally. She asks that we come and do things *with* the kids rather than *for* them. "And don't worry too much about how much spoiling may go on. We'll straighten all that out when you go back home." This is the happiest kind of welcome mat, which, sincerely expressed, makes grandparenting something of what it ought to be—a rich dividend, a golden reward for the golden years.

All this relates to your role as grandparent: how can you and I expect to be welcome and interesting to any of the younger people in our lives if we bring only downcast, despairing and dark moments and memories? *Handle your hurts privately and strongly;* bring new ideas and create new memories and you will be welcome forever—and missed for a very long time after you have gone.

Grandparents are, indeed, such a *natural* resource. But they do seem to be, too much, somewhere else. Sociologists decry this new reality. Gone is the wonderful and trusted sharing of old values which have weathered well, especially those values which loom largest and soundest when viewed through the lens of longer perspectives.

Last week, I saw both a TV message and a newspaper ad which showed and told how grandparents could make a small gift now and look ahead to problems solved for their grandchildren years in the future. For example, the newspaper ad suggests:

First Grandchild? Make An Investment In Her Future!

Help assure advanced schooling, a business start, a far-off wedding, or homebuying funds. Money invested in our $1,000 mini-

mum, 4-year savings certificates more than doubles in ten years,
based on earnings at our 7½% current rate compounded daily.
(*1978 data.)*

Invest now:	Get back in 4 years*	Get back in 10 years*
$ 1,000	$ 1,355.46	$ 2,139.02
3,000	4,066.38	6,417.06
5,000	6,777.30	10,695.10
10,000	13,554.60	21,390.20

Plan and chart based on investment of $1,000 minimum, 4-year savings certificates paying 7½% compounded daily. The Grandparent Plan sends your love ahead—and doubles in helping power in ten years. (1978 data.)

The TV message told much the same thing, *plus this idea:* "If you invest $1,000 in a savings certificate, at a grandchild's birth, that grandchild would have—by the time of retirement at age 65—$140,000 and then some. The magic secret of compound interest!

There is a new problem on the horizon. You meet more and more people who are worried that they will never become grandparents because young people are marrying later, and having their children later, if they are having any at all. It may be that we will, in time, lose even more of the blessed providence of grandparent power and that it won't be so much a wasted natural resource as an obsolete one.

Milt Erickson is a retired merchant who owned and operated a half dozen stores somewhere in the middle of Michigan. It may not be exactly correct to say that he had operated them; he still hovers around the fringes to keep himself busy. He told me candidly, and quite innocently, how he had turned over the stores to his hardworking and very promising son, George. Milt laughed: he recently exacted a promise from George to get him to stop being so hardworking; the old man worries about his hustling and hungry, and never-quitting son. Milt has several daughters and at least two of these are married and have children of their own. So Milton is a grandfather.

Erickson is bald and soft-spoken but he is not without vigorous feelings about things he feels strongly about. He admitted, for example, that he is setting up trusts so that some of his success might be shared with his daughters while they are still struggling with young families. These trusts were set up thoughtfully and carefully because Milt recognizes a current phenomenon. He is not unaware that many marriages today end in divorce, and by all odds, that might also happen in his family. He didn't want to be leaving substantial monies to any of these daughters for his grandchildren when (if there should be a divorce, heaven forbid) some of that money might go through the children to some guy he cared nothing about. Milt Erickson is a realist and a prudent man. The trusts he set up for his daughters, and for each of the grandchildren, were principally to provide for the children's education, but they have other potential purposes for later in life. He smiled when he told me that he gave the stores to his son, turning over his money machine and all of the hard work of that, to his principal heir apparent. The girls get their money, now.

"Me," Milt continued, "I like a little sensible squandering. Sharing it around and using a little of it—makes me feel like all that hard work was really okay. But I guess women carry a higher apprehension. Not all women, to be sure, but my wife apparently does. So we don't go very far and we stay deeply involved with our families and I guess that's okay. I get to baseball and football games when I want to and still go fishing with some of my buddies.

"Speaking of old buddies, I had a call awhile ago from an old business friend named Tim Flynn. We've called him Skin Flynn for years. And now that he's bald like me, it's probably not funny anymore, but we still call him that.

"When Skin called me—he always comes on straight and strong—he told me to buy Boeing.

"I said, 'What for? What's Boeing been doing lately?'

"Skin told me that they were in what's called a turnaround situation in the stock market; they had had real bad times back there with those big super jets and all. Lots of cash-flow problems several years ago and high developmental costs that had got way out of hand, some of it on the damn, screwed-up government busi-

ness. But, they're in a real turnaround now. 'So, Milt, you better buy some Boeing.'

'' 'Skin', I challenged him, 'Did you ever have a ride on one?'

'' 'On a jet plane, Milt? You nuts?' Skin was coming on strong again. 'Hell, I ain't got no time to go flyin' around the country in those damn jet airplanes. I got to keep sittin' right here keepin' track of my investments. It's a full time job for me, Milt. Lots to look after; mistakes to watch out for; got to keep it moving or it'll all go to hell like everything else,' shouts Skin.

"Listen, you old skinhead, it's about time—and you and I are about the same age, 75 or so; I think it's about time you picked up one of those grandchildren down there in Cleveland or Cincinnati or wherever it is they live. Take 'em for a ride on a super jet, on a Boeing, and fly off to Houston or Dallas or wherever it is that your other son lives and has his family. Get those grandchildren together so they get to know each other and so they get to know you a little bit, you old Scrooge! It's time you got to know 'em and share a little of yourself with 'em—while you're still alive, Skin! Besides your grandkids ought to get to know each other if all of our past and prudent carefulness has ever been worth a damn. Better show 'em to each other, and show 'em yourself as well. And talk to those kids, Skin, not about buying Boeing but about riding on 'em and enjoying 'em and getting somewhere as people, not just as penny-pinchin', preoccupied accumulators all the time. Then when you get done with that trip, you've got some more to take . . . down to Florida and out to California, and take your wife along and let her enjoy life a little instead of always sitting home watching you as you hide behind the Wall Street Journal and Forbes Magazine and all that other fiscal foolishness. Skin, I got the same financial problems you've got. We both got too successful and piled up more than we can use up. Sure we may be starting to think about how we can parcel it out among the kids but it comes too late for many of us and we share it stupidly—too often after we're gone, Skin. What kind of a respected memory can that be; or will it ever be?

"I think it would be a lot better if you and I could still learn a little about being people with these youngsters; we're partially

*responsible for them. I think we better bring 'em a little of our-
selves and bring a little of that bankroll along with us; we'd better
learn to enjoy sprinkling it around a little to see all those happy
people while they're still happy. It's getting so, Skin, that there
doesn't seem to be any fun anymore.*

*"Won't it be a laugh, Skin, when they inherit our money—
they won't be able to remember what the hell we look like; who
the hell we were. See you on one of those big Boeing jets one of
these days, Skin, and so long, Scrooge!"*

*Walter Rogers sent the plane tickets and made all other ar-
rangements—for a visit from two of his far-away grandchildren.
And, as soon as they got there, he had an immediate return on his
investment. The kids arrived wearing, not only name tags, but
more which read:*
  *"My name is Andy Rogers. I am going to Richmond, Virginia.
My grandfather is a big judge there."*
The other child's ID tag read:
  *"My name is Mindy Rogers. I am also going to Richmond. My
grandmother helps my grandfather because he is a big Democrat."*

It is not easy to be successful in the grandparent business these
days. In historic times, grandma escaped all this trauma of uncertainty
and all these tenuous role-playings. She was busy with her big family,
with her busy kitchen and with the eight-room house, and with all
those chickens and eggs and everything else that needed gathering and
fixing and fussing over from sun-up to sun-down and well beyond. If
there had been a late, late show then, grandma would have missed it
because she was still busy with the day's chores, and preparing for to-
morrow's. Grandma was lucky. She didn't have any leisure problems.
She wasn't bored. Overworked sometimes, perhaps, but bless her; she
was busy—and needed—and loved.

You cannot say with any certainty that you will never get married
again because you cannot know what is around life's corners.

*There is this candid, true tale of an eighty-five-year-old patient in
a nursing infirmary. One day, he preyed upon the "terminally-ill*

specialist'' begging that she should pray for him; that she should plead with God to take him out of his misery and out of his empty and finished life. He protested that God had stopped loving him anyway; there was so little time left and so little energy remaining. "Please, doctor, pray to God that I should die—soon!" He made the doctor promise.

The specialist walked away, nodding and absently agreeing, while off in concerned contact with still other patients with still other problems for which there were no better answers. These people were all old and terminal.

On a return visit a month later, the eighty-five-year-old man "nailed" the doctor with his admonishing questions:

"I asked you to pray to God that he should let me die, doctor! Did you say that prayer, doctor?"

The doctor stopped, remembering, and a touch embarrassed, admitted that she had become too busy with too many other patients and had simply forgotten her promise.

The eighty-five-year-old patient almost shouted: "Good! Good, doctor! I'm glad you forgot. You see, doctor, I met this seventy-three-year-old widow across the hall, and I can't die now."

9

Being of Sound Mind —Start Spending It

Anyone may so arrange his affairs that his taxes shall be as low as possible; he is not bound to choose that pattern which will best pay the Treasury; there is not even a patriotic duty to increase one's taxes.

JUDGE LEARNED HAND,
"Helvering vs. Gregory," 1934

Peter Henrikson, and his wife, Esther, are retired at one of those havens which beckon frost-bitten Northerners to the balmy coasts of the Carolina shores. Where the breezes are gentle and the outdoor living goes on year round. On a recent visit with one of their daughters, talk drifted around to money, to the cost of everything, and how terrible it all was. But this dialogue verified the long-held suspicion in that family that there were still plenty of assets.

"What are you hanging onto all those golden marbles for, Dad?" the well-liked son-in-law wanted to know. He also inquired, as if to remind the old folks. "How old are the two of you, now?"

"One's seventy-five going on eighty and the other one of us is the same," the old man joked. There was a mild twitter. Henrikson continued, "There have always been things we wanted, or wanted to do. We always hoped to go to Sweden where our parents came from, but it got so late, and now it costs so much. And, I always had an ambition to own a Cadillac, but Esther in-

sists that's putting on airs, even if we could afford it. But, what I really always wanted was a fine watch for myself." He stared off pensively.

"How much do you guess such a watch would cost, Dad?" his daughter wanted to know.

"Oh, hell, I'll bet that type of watch would cost all of a hundred dollars–or maybe more."

"Then, for heaven's sake, Dad, why don't you go down to-morrow, and get any watch your heart desires. Isn't it about time that you and Mom had what you want?" She said it both kindly, and firmly.

Peter Henrikson did get his watch, but the young people bet that he still bargained hard for it.

I've never heard the ancient Oriental proverb to say, "Much wisdom in Chinese fortune cookie." But there ought to be such a proverb, since my wife's holiday cookie message read, "Wealth belong to he who enjoy it."

Hank York never worked—never in all of his forty-five years. Hank's father worked hard, and he saved hard and invested shrewdly. Then he died and left a very fat estate residue which is still paying out plenty.

Hank has a monthly income from his father's estate of about three thousand dollars. That is $3,000, monthly. What does Hank do with the money and with his life? I heard him as he sat two stools away in his small town's "home-cooking, paper-napkin eatery." He haggled unpleasantly:*

"What's today's special? I mean your special special . . . and what are you going to stick me for it?"

More than ten years ago I checked, carefully and conservatively, with probate judges, estate planning attorneys, and other finance professionals, to try to determine what middle class and upper income persons were leaving behind in estate residues. At that time, I was assured that such ordinary people died and left at least $40,000 on average. That was ten years ago. The current, and most reliable data from a variety of sources, indicates that average estate leftovers now reach about $150,000. This is not only from the rich, or the large estates, but from white- and blue-collar families alike.

> *Then, there is Margaret Stevens who isn't loaded at all. She probably ought to show just a bit more sensible concern. When her lingering husband finally moved out to the cemetery, Margaret also moved. She sold the home they had long maintained, where their kids had grown up and moved out of town to be with her younger sister, Charlotte.*
>
> *Margaret easily made new friends, and a new life. She took up crafts, and oil painting. But Charlotte, the younger sister, had a stroke, and they moved her to a nursing home where the care might be more constant, if less loving. Margaret stays on in Charlotte's home, with the blessing of Charlotte's children, and everyone is waiting to see how this tangled life situation will get untangled. All but Margaret. At eighty-two, she walks where she can, or is picked up by friends, old and new. She visits others who are old and infirm or alone. She is good company, full of stories and tartly told tales about her grandfather, the undertaker.*
>
> *As concerns money matters, I am not sure whether the boys at IRS even know her name, or have her number. Perhaps, she is among that so-called "ordinary pile of common estate residues," which, by their own admission, goes largely unnoticed, and unchallenged by the estate and inheritance tax gentlemen.*
>
> *Margaret Stevens is not concerned about such things. She believes and demonstrates that, even at eighty-two, life is for living—and for the living.*

I saw an inspirational legend last week, one of those hand-lettered pieces; it was hanging on the wall behind a secretary's desk, in the trust department of a semimetropolitan bank. The message suggested, "It is not by hoarding wealth, or love, that man grows rich, I see. The more I freely give to life, the more life gives to me." And yet, despite all of our careful planning, things have a way of going awry. A stern warning is conveyed in this modern Greek tragedy:

> *Sal Halady became a fast friend with a man on his cruise as they luxuriated serenely throughout the Mediterranean, climbing all*

over antiquity in Greece, last year. They enjoyed most meals together, along with Sal's wife and the other guy's lady companion. On one of the last days, six o'clock in the morning, they met for breakfast, had their tour guide briefing, and climbed once more aboard the tour bus.

Ten minutes later, Sal's new friend was dead–on the bus–with an apparent heart attack. They were, as Sal explains, in the most primitive of villages; and they were detained there for five or more hours while official calls were made–to the U.S. embassy in Athens, to the State Department in Washington, and (at three in the morning) to the man's family in Peoria. After many such calls, and much language mystery, and after someone wired $3,000 to prepare the body, and to ship it back to America, the rest of the group was permitted to complete the tour. And the fellow's lady companion was finally permitted to accompany the body back home.

The message purely and simply is that you and I must always–and everywhere–have our "house," and every other damn thing, in neat, and official dying order. We need to carry with us names of family members or other persons to contact, and phone numbers and addresses. And we ought to try to have all this on our own person.

In the secure knowledge that this is in order, have a pleasant journey.

In one of his renowned platform appearances of some time ago, former President Sachar of Brandeis University is reported to have said:

"The trouble with today is that the future is not what it used to be. Our crisis is not one of death, decline, and disintegration, as described by Spengler. Rather, it is the greatest revolution in recorded history–a release of capacity and hope as no generation has known. But we cannot expect to live through it without travail and sacrifice. When pain disappears, death is near.

. . . We are children of the dusk–with one foot in a world that is going and one foot in a world that is coming. . . ."

As we settle in our minds and think ahead, we may contemplate our last day, our last hamburger, and we may grow apprehensive about timing. What if in our race leftovers are not running even with time? The trick, apparently, is to begin to nibble away at our golden goose very judiciously. Because we will want, at the same time, to keep that goose laying more of its golden eggs for our use and enjoyment. So slice a careful sliver here, and another there, but remember to pat and cajole your special goose—as long as you hope for more of those golden eggs. So then, blessings on you, my friends. Be of sound and happy minds as you start spending what you want to spend of what it is that you possess.

A final word:

> "He may not have taken it with him, but
> then he didn't get around to leaving
> it either—until it had become practically
> worthless."

Elmer Otte

SELECTED READINGS

Selected Readings

Abt Associates. Property tax relief programs for the elderly. Washington, D.C.: U.S. Government Printing Office, 1975.

Alpert, H. "Flexitime, flexiwork, flexijobs, and retiree job sharing." *Retirement Living* 17:22–25; May, 1977.

Annand, M. "Banking made easy—for the elderly. *Burroughs Clearing House* 59:26–27; February, 1975.

Ball, R. M. "Social security and private pension plans." *National Tax Journal* 27:467–471; September, 1974.

Barrett, A. "What you should know about pension plans." *Industrial Distribution* 62:27; May, 1972.

Bartlett, D. M. "Retirement counseling: making sure employees aren't dropouts." *Personnel* 51:26–35; November, 1974.

Bell, D. R. "Prevalence of private retirement plans." *Monthly Labor Review* 98:17–20; October, 1975.

Blake, J. "How much money do you need for retirement?" *American Druggist* 173:16; March, 1976.

Bland, D. "Over-50 job hunter up against the establishment." *Marketing Communications* 299:26–30; February, 1971.

Butler, P. "Pension: reward or right?" *Labour Gazette* 71:448–455; July, 1971.

Butler, P. "Problems of the older worker." *Labour Gazette* 70:775–782; November, 1970.

Carlson, C. and Guttentag, J. M. "Money and your home." *Retirement Living* 17:34; January, 1977.

Cody, D. D. "Outlook for the social security system." *Best's Review Life/Health Insurance Edition* 76:10; June, 1975.

Comleigh, I. U. "Income investing for the medicare set." *Commercial and Financial Chronicle* 216:684; September 7, 1972.

Davis, H. E. "Pension provisions affecting the employment of older workers." *Monthly Labor Review* 96:41–45; April, 1973.

Douglas, Paul H. *Social security in the United States: an analysis and appraisal of the federal social security act.* New York: Arno Press; 1971.

Edgerton, J. "Preserving assets for a secure retirement." *Money* 5:78–79; November, 1976.

Eriksen, E. G. "Budgeting in retirement." *Management Accounting* 56:54–56; April, 1975.

Feldstein, M. "Social security and saving: the extended life cycle theory." *American Economic Review* 66:77–86; May, 1976.

"Financial assets and homeownership of the aged." *Monthly Labor Review* 96:63; January, 1973.

Grad, S. "Economically dependent persons without pension coverage in old age." *Social Security Bulletin* 38:13–17; October, 1975.

Grad, S. "Relative importance of income sources of the ages." *Social Security Bulletin* 36:37–45; August, 1973.

Hallaire, J. "Part-time employment for older persons." *Labour Gazette* 71:124; February, 1971.

Harris, C. L. "Social security: problems of the longer run." *Trusts and Estates* 114:850–853; December, 1975.

"Jobs not pensions." *Forbes* 118:62; July 15, 1976.

Johnson, M. "Early retirees find inflation is modifying their plans." *Industry Week* 186:18–21; September 22, 1975.

Kagan, J. "How social security shortchanges women." *McCall's* 103:54; February, 1976.

Kolodrubetz, W. W. "Private retirement benefits and relationships to earnings: survey of new beneficiaries." *Social Security Bulletin* 36:16–37; May 23, 1973.

Korns, Alexander. "Issue in financing retirement." Washington: U.S. Government Printing Office, December, 1976.

Koslow, S. P. "Jobscope: banking your future; IRA program and Keogh plan." *Mademoiselle* 82:244; September, 1976.

Laufer, A. C. and Fawler Jr., W. M. "Work potential of the aging." *Personnel Administration* 34:20–25; March, 1971.

LeBreton, Edmons. *Plan your retirement now so you won't be sorry later.* New York: U.S. News and World Report, 1975.

Lesnoy, S. D. "Social security, saving, and capital formation." *Social Security Bulletin* 38:3–15; July, 1975.

Main, Jeremy. "The good life costs less after 65." *Money* 2:70–75; May, 1973.

Mallan, L. B. "Women born in the early 1900's: employment, earnings, and benefit levels." *Social Security Bulletin,* 37:3–25; March, 1974.

Mallan, L. B. "Women's worklives and future social security benefits." *Social Security Bulletin* 39:3–13; April, 1976.

"Mammoth new tax reform bill expands some deductions, shrinks some loopholes: changes for retirees." *Retirement Living* 16:11–12; November, 1976.

Masse, B. L. "Penalizing the oldsters' earnings." *America* 122:119; February 7, 1970.

Meisenberg, S. "Can I lose my pension benefits after paying into a fund?" *Harvest Years* 12:51–52; January, 1972.

Merrion, P. R. "Self-insurance funds may be allowed by hospital Medicare refund rules." *Business Insurance* 10:8; August 9, 1976.

Messinger, R. "Set up your own retirement plan." *McCall's* 102:39; September, 1975.

Murray, J. "Activities and expenditures of preretirees." *Social Security Bulletin* 38:5–21; August, 1975.

Murray, J. "Homeownership and financial assets: findings from the 1968 survey of the aged." *Social Security Bulletin* 35:3–23; August, 1972.

Myers, R. I. "Financing social security—how?" *National Underwriter Life and Health Insurance Edition* 79:24–25; September, 1975.

Myers, R. I. "Reappraisal of the basic purpose of social security." *CLU Journal* 31:35–41; January, 1977.

Nader, R. "How you lose money by being a woman: plight of the aged." *McCall's* 99:65; January, 1972.

Nader, Ralph. *You and your pension.* New York: Grossman Publishers, Inc., 1972.

"New retirement plans make taking it easy, easier." *Chemical Week* 107:31–33; November 11, 1970.

"New tax law carries provisions to aid elderly." *Aging* 247:4; May, 1975.

"Planning for retirement." *Business Week* pp. 75–81; August 18, 1973.

Porter, S. "Economics of Retirement: excerpt from *Sylvia Porter's Money Book.*" *Today's Education* 65:64–66; January, 1976.

Porter, S. "Spending your money: individual retirement accounts for homemakers." *Ladies Home Journal* 94:31; March, 1977.

"Practical use for the private annuity." *CPA Journal* 46:50; January, 1976.

"Retirement: how to start planning in your 30's and 40's." *Changing Times* 30:20–24; June, 1976.

"Retirement: what to do if you're in your 50's?" *Changing Times* 30:43–47; July, 1976.

Samuelson, P. A. "Financing pensions." *Newsweek* 89:62; April 4, 1977.

Swartz, Melvin J. *Don't die broke: a guide to secure retirement.* Riverside, N.J.: Macmillan Publishing Company, Inc., 1975.

INDEX

Index